THE ULTIMATE NINJA CREAMI COOKBOOK

1500 Days of Perfect and Indulgent Ice Creams, Gelato, Sorbet, Shakes, Smoothies, and Other Frozen Treats. | Full-Color Picture Premium Edition.

EVE P. HOGAN

EDITOR: LYN

INTERIOR DESIGN: FAIZAN

COVER ART: ABR

FOOD STYLIST: JO

Table of Contents

Ninja Creami is a brand of kitchen appliances that specializes in making delicious frozen treats like ice cream, gelato, sorbet, and more. It allows you to create your own custom flavors and experiment with various ingredients to make creamy and flavorful desserts right at home.

The Ninja Creami machines typically come with a variety of settings and attachments to help you achieve the perfect texture and consistency for your frozen treats. They often feature powerful blending and mixing capabilities, allowing you to whip up creamy creations in a matter of minutes.

With Ninja Creami, you have the flexibility to control the ingredients and customize your desserts according to your preferences. You can choose to make healthier versions using fresh fruits and low-sugar options or indulge in decadent flavors by adding your favorite mix-ins and toppings.

Overall, Ninja Creami offers a convenient and fun way to satisfy your sweet tooth and enjoy homemade frozen treats without the need for specialized equipment or lengthy preparation. It's a great addition to any kitchen for those who love experimenting with flavors and creating their own delightful frozen desserts.

Main Components and Design

The Ninja Creami machine consists of several main components that contribute to its functionality and design. Here are the main components and an overview of their roles:

BASE UNIT

The base unit serves as the foundation of the Ninja Creami machine.

It houses the motor and control panel, providing power and control over the machine's functions.

BLENDER ATTACHMENT

The blender attachment is a removable component that connects to the base unit.

It consists of a blending pitcher or container, blades, and a lid.

This attachment is responsible for mixing and blending the ingredients to create smooth and creamy textures.

FREEZING BOWL

The freezing bowl is an essential component that is placed in the freezer prior to use.

It is typically made of a durable material, such as stainless steel or a double-walled container, to facilitate even freezing.

The freezing bowl needs to be properly chilled to the recommended temperature before adding ingredients.

PADDLES AND WHISKS

The Ninja Creami machine often includes different types of paddles and whisks that attach to the blender attachment.

These attachments help incorporate air into the mixture and aid in achieving the desired consistency for various frozen treats.

Paddles are typically used for ice cream and gelato-like creations, while whisks are suitable for lighter and fluffier desserts.

CONTROL PANEL

The control panel is located on the base unit and provides the interface for operating the Ninja Creami machine.

It typically consists of buttons, dials, and a display screen.

The control panel allows you to select different settings, adjust time and speed, and monitor the progress of your frozen treat preparation.

STORAGE CONTAINERS

The Ninja Creami machine often comes with storage containers for storing the prepared frozen treats.

These containers are designed to fit the machine's output and provide a convenient way to store excess or leftover desserts.

The design of the Ninja Creami machine is usually sleek, compact, and user-friendly. It aims to provide a seamless experience for creating homemade frozen treats with ease. The components are designed to be detachable for easy cleaning and maintenance. The machine's aesthetic and functionality make it an attractive addition to any kitchen countertop.

PRE-FREEZE THE FREEZING BOWL

Ensure the freezing bowl is properly chilled before using it. Place it in the freezer for the recommended amount of time (usually overnight) to achieve the ideal temperature for freezing.

USE COLD INGREDIENTS

For best results, use ingredients that are already chilled or cold. This helps the freezing process and promotes faster and smoother freezing of the mixture.

ADD MIX-INS AT THE RIGHT TIME

If you're incorporating mix-ins like chocolate chips, nuts, or fruits, add them during the last few minutes of the freezing process. This allows them to be evenly distributed without sinking to the bottom.

EXPERIMENT WITH TEXTURE

Adjust the freezing time to achieve your desired texture. For softer and creamier results, reduce the freezing time slightly. For firmer and harder consistency, increase the freezing time.

AVOID OVERFILLING

Be mindful of the maximum capacity of the blending pitcher or container. Overfilling may result in overflow or uneven freezing. Follow the recommended guidelines for each recipe or the capacity indicated by the manufacturer.

LAYER FLAVORS

Create layered or swirled frozen treats by freezing different flavors separately and then combining them in layers. Alternate pouring different mixtures into the freezing bowl to create visually appealing and tasty combinations.

EXPERIMENT WITH FLAVORS AND ADD-INS

Don't be afraid to get creative with your flavor combinations and mix-ins. Experiment with different fruits, extracts, spices, and even small candies or cookies to personalize your frozen treats.

CLEAN IMMEDIATELY

After using the Ninja Creami machine, clean the blending pitcher, attachments, and freezing bowl promptly. This ensures that residue doesn't harden and makes cleaning easier. Follow the manufacturer's instructions for cleaning and maintenance.

PLAN AHEAD

If you have specific dessert plans or gatherings, plan ahead and prepare the frozen treats in advance. Some recipes may require longer freezing times or additional chilling time before serving.

Enjoy Freshly Made Treats

Frozen treats made with the Ninja Creami are best enjoyed immediately after preparation. The texture and consistency are often at their peak right after freezing, providing the ultimate indulgence.

Troubleshooting and FAQs

TROUBLESHOOTING:

Issue: The mixture is not freezing or taking too long to freeze.

Solution: Ensure that the freezing bowl is properly pre-frozen for the recommended time. Check that the ingredients are cold or chilled before adding them to the machine. Adjust the freezing time or temperature settings if necessary.

Issue: The mixture is not achieving the desired consistency.

Solution: Make sure to follow the recipe instructions and measurements accurately. Adjust the blending time or use different paddle attachments to achieve the desired consistency. Experiment with the texture by varying the freezing time.

Issue: The machine is not turning on or operating.

Solution: Check that the machine is properly plugged in and the power source is functioning. Ensure that all attachments are securely attached to the base unit. Refer to the user manual for any specific troubleshooting steps.

Issue: Excessive noise or vibration during operation.

Solution: Ensure that all components and attachments are properly assembled and securely in place. Check for any obstructions or foreign objects that might be causing the noise or vibration. Contact customer support if the issue persists.

FREQUENTLY ASKED QUESTIONS (FAQS):

Can I make dairy-free or vegan frozen treats with the Ninja Creami?

Yes, the Ninja Creami can be used to create dairy-free or vegan frozen treats. Simply use alternative milk options such as almond milk, coconut milk, or soy milk, and substitute ingredients accordingly.

Can I make large batches of frozen treats with the Ninja Creami?

The capacity of the Ninja Creami machine may vary, but it is typically designed for moderate-sized batches. It is recommended to follow the recommended capacity guidelines provided by the manufacturer.

How long does it typically take to freeze the mixture?

The freezing time can vary depending on the recipe, desired texture, and the temperature of the ingredients. On average, freezing times can range from 15 to 30 minutes, but it's important to refer to the specific recipe instructions for accurate timings.

Can I use the Ninja Creami for purposes other than making frozen treats?

The Ninja Creami is primarily designed for making frozen treats. While it may have additional functions, it's best to consult the user manual or contact the manufacturer for guidance on using it for other purposes.

Chapter 2
Getting Started with Ninja Creami

Basic Ingredients for Creating Amazing Frozen Treats

DAIRY

Heavy cream: Provides richness and creaminess to ice cream and gelato.

Milk: Helps create a smooth and pourable base for frozen treats.

Yogurt: Adds tanginess and a creamy texture to frozen yogurt.

SWEETENERS

Sugar: Adds sweetness to balance the flavors in your frozen treats.

Honey: Provides natural sweetness and enhances flavors.

Maple syrup: Adds a distinct flavor profile and sweetness.

FRUITS

Fresh fruits: Use a variety of fruits such as berries, peaches, mangoes, and bananas to add natural flavors, sweetness, and texture.

Fruit purees: Pureed fruits can be used to infuse flavor throughout the frozen treat.

FLAVORS AND EXTRACTS

Vanilla extract: Enhances the overall flavor of your frozen treats.

Almond extract, mint extract, or other flavorings: Add unique and distinct flavors to your creations.

MIX-INS AND TOPPINGS

Chocolate chips, nuts, and candies: Add texture and bursts of flavor to your frozen treats.

Cookie crumbs, brownie bits, or cake pieces: Create delightful layers and add extra indulgence.

Whipped cream, chocolate sauce, caramel sauce, or fruit compote: Perfect for topping off your frozen treats and adding a finishing touch.

OPTIONAL ADDITIONS

Spices and herbs: Experiment with flavors like cinnamon, nutmeg, or basil for an interesting twist.

Coffee or tea: Infuse your frozen treats with the flavors of your favorite brew.

Liqueurs or spirits: Add a touch of adult sophistication and unique flavors to your creations (optional and for adults only).

Mastering the Art of Frozen Treats

Creating homemade frozen treats is a delightful journey that allows you to express your culinary creativity and indulge in sweet, creamy delights. To truly master the art of frozen treats, it takes a combination of technique, imagination, and a passion for experimentation. With your Ninja Creami machine as your trusted companion, you have the tools to elevate your skills and create frozen masterpieces that will impress family and friends. Let's embark on this flavorful adventure and unlock the secrets to mastering the art of frozen treats.

PERFECTING THE BASE

At the heart of every great frozen treat is a perfectly balanced base. Whether you're making ice cream, gelato, or frozen yogurt, nailing the base is essential. Experiment with different ratios of dairy, sugar, and flavors to achieve the ideal taste and texture. Take note of the nuances in each ingredient and how they contribute to the final result. Harness the power of your Ninja Creami machine to blend and mix the base ingredients to perfection, ensuring a smooth and creamy consistency that will have everyone begging for seconds.

EXPERIMENTING WITH FLAVORS

One of the joys of mastering frozen treats is the ability to experiment with an array of flavors. From classic favorites to bold and innovative combinations, the possibilities are endless. Start by exploring traditional flavors like vanilla, chocolate, and strawberry, and then branch out into more exotic options like lavender honey, chai spice, or salted caramel. Don't be afraid to get adventurous and infuse your creations with unexpected ingredients like herbs, spices, or even a touch of your favorite liqueur. Let your taste buds guide you on a flavor adventure that will captivate and surprise.

PERFECTING THE TEXTURE

Texture plays a crucial role in the enjoyment of frozen treats. Achieving a velvety smooth texture or a delightful lightness requires attention to detail. Experiment with different freezing times, mixing techniques, and the use of paddles and whisks to create the desired consistency. Take the time to understand how each attachment and technique influences the texture and experiment to find the perfect balance for your preferences. Whether you prefer a dense and creamy ice cream or a light and airy frozen yogurt, mastering the texture will elevate your frozen treats to new heights.

PLAYING WITH MIX-INS AND TOPPINGS

Adding mix-ins and toppings to your frozen treats is a wonderful way to enhance flavors and create delightful surprises. From chunks of chocolate and swirls of caramel to crunchy nuts and vibrant fruits, the options are endless. Experiment with different combinations, textures, and ratios to strike the perfect balance. Remember to consider the size and texture of your mix-ins to ensure they complement the base and freeze uniformly. Let your creativity shine as you play with different combinations and discover the joy of that first bite.

PRESENTATION AND GARNISHES

Mastering the art of frozen treats extends beyond the flavors and textures—it also involves presenting your creations in an enticing and visually appealing manner. Pay attention to plating techniques, garnishes, and serving vessels to create a feast for the eyes. Whether it's a simple scoop elegantly placed in a bowl, a towering sundae adorned with whipped cream and a cherry on top, or a beautifully layered parfait, presentation can elevate the experience and make your frozen treats even more enticing.

Keep Dreaming and Creaming

In the world of frozen treats, the possibilities are endless. With your Ninja Creami machine, you have unlocked a world of creamy, dreamy delights right in your own kitchen. But the journey doesn't end there. As you continue to explore and create, there's no limit to the delectable frozen concoctions you can bring to life. So, let's dive into the world of "Keep Dreaming and Creaming" and discover how you can continue to indulge your taste buds and feed your imagination.

UNLEASH YOUR CREATIVITY

The beauty of owning a Ninja Creami machine is that it empowers you to experiment and unleash your creativity. Don't be afraid to dream big and think outside the box. Mix and match flavors, try new ingredients, and push the boundaries of what's possible. Whether you're crafting classic favorites or inventing unique flavor combinations, the key is to let your imagination run wild. The result? Frozen treats that are uniquely yours, reflecting your personal style and culinary prowess.

ELEVATE YOUR TECHNIQUES

As you delve deeper into the world of frozen treats, take the opportunity to refine your techniques and expand your skill set. Experiment with different freezing times to achieve varying consistencies. Master the art of swirling and layering flavors to create stunning visual appeal. Play with different attachments and tools provided with your Ninja Creami machine to achieve the perfect texture and taste. By continuously honing your skills, you'll elevate your frozen creations to new heights and amaze yourself and your loved ones with your culinary prowess.

EMBRACE SEASONAL INSPIRATIONS

One of the joys of creating frozen treats is the ability to embrace the changing seasons and the flavors they bring. From refreshing fruity sorbets in the summer to indulgent spiced creations in the fall, let the seasons guide your inspiration. Seek out the freshest produce, experiment with seasonal spices and flavors, and celebrate the unique offerings of each time of year. By embracing seasonal inspirations, you'll keep your creations fresh, exciting, and perfectly in tune with the spirit of the season.

SHARE THE JOY

Frozen treats have a magical way of bringing people together and spreading joy. As you continue dreaming and creaming, don't forget to share your creations with others. Whether it's hosting a frozen treat party, surprising a friend with a personalized flavor, or simply delighting your loved ones with a homemade dessert, the act of sharing adds an extra layer of fulfillment to your culinary adventures. Let the joy of your creations be a source of happiness and connection with those around you.

With every frozen treat you create, the journey of dreaming and creaming continues. The Ninja Creami machine is your trusted companion, unlocking endless possibilities for delicious and imaginative creations. So, keep dreaming big, pushing the boundaries, and feeding your passion for frozen delights. With every scoop, you're not only indulging your taste buds but also nourishing your creativity and bringing a touch of magic to your kitchen. Keep dreaming and creaming, and let your frozen creations be a reflection of the joy and wonder that comes from embracing the art of dessert making.

Chapter 3
Ice Cream Mix-ins

Chocolate Brownie Ice Cream

Prep time: 5 minutes | Cook time: 3 minutes | Serves 4

- 1 tablespoon cream cheese, softened
- ⅓ cup granulated sugar
- 1 teaspoon vanilla extract
- 2 tablespoons cocoa powder
- 1 cup whole milk
- ¾ cup heavy cream
- 2 tablespoons mini chocolate chips
- 2 tablespoons brownie chunks

1. In a large microwave-safe bowl, add the cream cheese and microwave on High for about ten seconds.
2. Remove from the microwave and stir until smooth.
3. Add the sugar and almond extract and with a wire whisk, beat until the mixture looks like frosting.
4. Slowly add the milk and heavy cream and beat until well combined.
5. Transfer the mixture into an empty Ninja CREAMi pint container.
6. Cover the container with storage lid and freeze for 24 hours.
7. After 24 hours, remove the lid from container and arrange into the Outer Bowl of Ninja CREAMi.
8. Install the Creamerizer Paddle onto the lid of Outer Bowl.
9. Then rotate the lid clockwise to lock.
10. Press Power button to turn on the unit.
11. Then press Ice Cream button.
12. When the program is completed, with a spoon, create a 1½-inch wide hole in the center that reaches the bottom of the pint container.
13. Add the chocolate chunks and brownie pieces into the hole and press Mix-In button. When the program is completed, turn the Outer Bowl and release it from the machine.
14. Transfer the ice cream into serving bowls and serve immediately.

Lavender Cookies & Cream Ice Cream

Prep time: 20 minutes | Cook time: 20 minutes | Freeze time: 24 hours | Serves 2

- ½ cup heavy cream
- ½ tablespoon dried culinary lavender
- ¼ teaspoon kosher salt
- ½ cup whole milk
- ¼ cup sweetened condensed milk
- 2 drops purple food coloring
- ¼ cup crushed chocolate wafer cookies

1. Whisk together the heavy cream, lavender, and salt in a medium saucepan.
2. Steep the mixture for 10 minutes over low heat, stirring every 2 minutes to prevent bubbling.
3. Using a fine-mesh strainer, drain the lavender from the heavy cream into a large mixing basin.

Discard the lavender.

4. Combine the milk, sweetened condensed milk, and purple food coloring in a large mixing bowl. Whisk until the mixture is completely smooth.
5. Pour the base into an empty CREAMi Pint. Place the Pint into an ice bath. Once cooled, place the storage lid on the Pint and freeze for 24 hours.
6. Remove the Pint from the freezer and remove its lid. Place Pint in outer bowl, install Creamerizer Paddle in outer bowl lid, and lock the lid assembly onto the outer bowl. Select ICE CREAM.
7. When the process is done, create a 1½-inch wide hole that reaches the bottom of the Pint with a spoon. It's okay if your treat exceeds the max fill line. Add crushed wafer cookies to the hole and process again using the MIX-IN program.
8. When processing is complete, remove ice cream from Pint and serve immediately, topped with extra crumbled wafers if desired.

Coconut Caramel Ice Cream

Prep time: 5 minutes | Cook time: 5 minutes | Serves 4

- 6 frozen bananas, peeled
- 1 bag fresh frozen coconut
- 1 teaspoon pure coconut extract
- 1 teaspoon brown sugar substitute
- 2 teaspoons pure vanilla extract
- 1/4 cup calorie free caramel sauce

1. Place a large mixing bowl under the Yonanas chute and push the bananas and coconut through.
2. Add coconut extract, vanilla extract and brown sugar substitute to the mixing bowl.
3. Mix until smooth.
4. Spoon into individual bowls.
5. Top with caramel sauce.
6. Freeze leftovers in an airtight container.

Tahini and Lemon Curd Ice Cream

Prep time: 5 minutes | Cook time: 5 minutes | Serves 4

- 12 frozen bananas, peeled
- 1/2 cup tahini paste
- 2 teaspoons pure vanilla extract
- 3 tablespoons lemon curd
- 1 teaspoon honey

1. Place a mixing bowl under the Yonanas chute and push the bananas through.
2. Add tahini, vanilla extract, lemon curd and honey to the mixing bowl.
3. Blend until smooth.
4. Spoon into individual bowls and freeze leftover soft-serve in an airtight container.

Fruity Cereal Ice Cream

Prep time: 30 minutes | Cook time: 30 minutes | Freeze time: 24 hours | Serves 2

- ¾ cup whole milk
- 1 cup fruity cereal, divided
- 1 tablespoon Philadelphia cream cheese, softened
- ¼ cup granulated sugar
- 1 teaspoon vanilla extract
- ½ cup heavy cream

1. In a large mixing bowl, combine ½ cup of the fruity cereal and the milk. Allow the mixture to settle for 15–30 minutes, stirring occasionally to infuse the milk with the fruity taste.
2. Microwave the Philadelphia cream cheese for 10 seconds in a second large microwave-safe dish. Combine the sugar and vanilla extract in a mixing bowl with a whisk or rubber spatula until the mixture resembles frosting, about 60 seconds.
3. After 15 to 30 minutes, sift the milk and cereal into the bowl with the sugar mixture using a fine-mesh filter. To release extra milk, press on the cereal with a spoon, then discard it. Mix in the heavy cream until everything is thoroughly mixed.
4. Pour the mixture into an empty ninja CREAMi Pint container. Add the strawberries to the Pint, making sure not to go over the max fill line, and freeze for 24 hours.
5. After 24 hours, remove the Pint from the freezer. Remove the lid.
6. Place the Ninja CREAMi Pint into the outer bowl. Place the outer bowl with the Pint in it into the ninja CREAMi machine and turn until the outer bowl locks into place. Push the ICE CREAM button. During the ICE CREAM function, the ice cream will mix together and become very creamy.
7. Use a spoon to create a 1½-inch wide hole that reaches the bottom of the Pint. Add the remaining ½ cup of fruity cereal to the hole and process again using the mix-in.When processing is complete, remove the ice cream from the Pint.

Bourbon-Maple-Walnut Ice Cream

Prep time: 15 minutes | Cook time: 5 minutes | Freeze time: 24 hours | Serves 4

- 4 large egg yolks
- ¼ cup maple syrup
- ¼ cup corn syrup
- 2 tablespoons bourbon
- ½ cup whole milk
- 1 cup heavy (whipping) cream
- ¼ cup toasted walnut halves

1. Fill a large bowl with ice water and set it aside.
2. In a small saucepan, whisk together the egg yolks, maple syrup, corn syrup, and bourbon until the mixture is fully combined. Do not do this over heat.
3. Whisk in the milk and heavy cream.
4. Place the pan over medium heat. Cook, stirring constantly with a rubber spatula, until the temperature reaches 165°F to 175°F on an instant-read thermometer.
5. Remove the pan from the heat and pour the base into a clean CREAMi Pint. Carefully place the container in the prepared ice water bath, making sure the water doesn't spill into the base.
6. Once the base has cooled, place the storage lid on the pint and freeze for 24 hours.
7. Remove the pint from the freezer and take off the lid. Place the pint in the outer bowl of your Ninja® CREAMi™, install the Creamerizer™ Paddle in the outer bowl lid, and lock the lid assembly onto the outer bowl. Place the bowl assembly on the motor base, and twist the handle to the right to raise the platform and lock it in place. Select the Ice Cream function.
8. Once the machine has finished processing, remove the lid from the pint container. With a spoon, create a 1½-inch-wide hole that reaches the bottom of the pint. During this process, it is okay if your treat reaches above the Max Fill line. Add the toasted walnuts to the hole in the pint, replace the lid, and select the Mix-In function.
9. Once the machine has finished processing, remove the ice cream from the pint. Serve immediately.

Sneaky Mint Chip Ice Cream

Prep time: 15 minutes | Cook time: 5 minutes | Freeze time: 24 hours | Serves 4

- 3 large egg yolks
- 1 tablespoon corn syrup
- ¼ cup granulated sugar
- ⅓ cup whole milk
- ¾ cup heavy (whipping) cream
- 1 cup packed fresh spinach
- ½ cup frozen peas, thawed
- 1 teaspoon mint extract
- ¼ cup semisweet chocolate chips

1. Fill a large bowl with ice water and set it aside.
2. In a small saucepan, whisk together the egg yolks, corn syrup, and sugar until the mixture is fully combined and the sugar is dissolved. Do not do this over heat.
3. Whisk in the milk and heavy cream.
4. Place the pan over medium heat. Cook, stirring constantly with a rubber spatula, until the temperature reaches 165°F to 175°F on an instant-read thermometer.
5. Remove the pan from the heat and pour the base into a clean CREAMi Pint. Carefully place the container in the prepared ice water bath, making sure the water doesn't spill into the base.
6. Once the mixture has completely cooled, pour the base into a blender and add the spinach, peas, and mint extract. Blend on high for 30 seconds. Strain the base through a fine-mesh strainer back into the CREAMi Pint. Place the storage lid on the container and freeze for 24 hours.
7. Remove the pint from the freezer and take off the lid. Place the pint in the outer bowl of your Ninja® CREAMi™, install the Creamerizer™ Paddle in the outer bowl lid, and lock the lid assembly onto the outer bowl. Place the bowl assembly on the motor base, and twist the handle to the right to raise the platform and lock it in place. Select the Ice Cream function.
8. Once the machine has finished processing, remove the lid from the pint container. With a spoon, create a 1½-inch-wide hole that reaches the bottom of the pint. During this process, it is okay if your treat reaches above the Max Fill line. Add the chocolate chips to the hole in the pint, replace the lid, and select the Mix-In function.
9. Once the machine has finished processing, remove the ice cream from the pint. Serve immediately.

Chocolate Malted Whopper Ice Cream

Prep time: 5 minutes | Cook time: 5 minutes | Serves 3-5

- 10 frozen bananas, peeled
- 1 cup coconut cream, chilled
- 1 tablespoon honey
- 1 teaspoon vanilla
- 1/2 cup Whoppers or chocolate covered malted milk balls

1. Place a mixing bowl under the Yonanas chute and push the bananas through.
2. Add coconut cream, honey and vanilla extract to the mixing bowl.
3. Blend until smooth.
4. Fold in whoppers, and spoon into individual servings.

Chocolate Coffee Ice Cream

Prep time: 2 hours 5 minutes | Cook time: 5 minutes | Serves 2-4

- 9 frozen bananas, peeled
- 1 cup Greek yogurt
- 2 tablespoons coffee
- 1 tablespoon brown sugar substitute
- 1/4 cup chocolate covered espresso beans, chopped

1. Whip the Greek yogurt with coffee and brown sugar substitute.
2. Place in the refrigerator for 2 hours to set.
3. Place a large mixing bowl under the Yonanas chute and push the bananas through.
4. Fold the coffee yogurt into the mixing bowl.
5. Mix until smooth.
6. Spoon into individual bowls and top with chocolate covered espresso beans.
7. Freeze leftovers in an airtight container.

Coffee And Cookies Ice Cream

Prep time: 5 minutes | Cook time: 3 minutes | Serves 4

- 1 tablespoon cream cheese, at room temperature
- ⅓ cup granulated sugar
- 1 teaspoon vanilla extract
- 1 tablespoon instant espresso
- ¾ cup heavy (whipping) cream
- 1 cup whole milk
- ¼ cup crushed chocolate sandwich cookies

1. In a large bowl, whisk together the cream cheese, sugar, and vanilla for about 1 minute, until the mixture looks like frosting.
2. Slowly whisk in the instant espresso, heavy cream, and milk until fully combined.
3. Pour the base into a clean CREAMi Pint. Place the lid on the container and freeze for 24 hours.
4. Remove the pint from the freezer and take off the lid. Place the pint in the outer bowl of your Ninja CREAMi, install the Creamerizer Paddle in the outer bowl lid, and lock the lid assembly onto the outer bowl. Place the bowl assembly on the motor base, and twist the handle to the right to raise the platform and lock it in place. Select the Ice Cream function.
5. Once the machine has finished processing, remove the lid from the pint container. With a spoon, create a 1½-inch-wide hole that reaches the bottom of the pint. Add the crushed cookies to the hole, replace the lid, and select the Mix-In function.
6. Once the machine has finished processing, remove the ice cream from the pint. Serve immediately.

Brownie Batter No-Churn Ice Cream

Prep time: 2 hours 5 minutes | Cook time: 5 minutes | Serves 2-4

- 9 frozen bananas, peeled
- 1/2 cup Greek Yogurt, vanilla flavored
- 1 teaspoon cocoa powder
- 2 gluten free brownies, chopped

1. Whip the Greek yogurt with cocoa powder
2. Place in the refrigerator for 2 hours to set.
3. Place a large mixing bowl under the Yonanas chute and push the bananas through.
4. Fold the chocolate yogurt into the soft-serve.
5. Mix until smooth.
6. Add brownie bites and mix delicately.
7. Spoon into individual bowls and freeze leftovers in an airtight container.

Chocolate Nut Ice Cream

Prep time: 10 minutes | Cook time: 10 minutes | Freeze time: 24 hours | Serves 6

- 1 cup whole milk
- ¾ cup heavy cream
- ⅓ cup granulated sugar
- 2 tablespoons mini chocolate chips
- 2 tablespoons cocoa powder
- ½ cup brownies, chopped
- ½ cup walnuts, chopped

1. Place the ingredients in a blender. Mix well until smooth.
2. Pour the mixture into the Ninja CREAMi Pint and close it with the lid.
3. Place the pint into the freezer and freeze for 24 hours.
4. Once done, open the lid and set the pint into the outer bowl of the Ninja CREAMi. Place the Creamerizer Paddle into the outer bowl.
5. Lock the lid by rotating it clockwise.
6. Turn on the unit and then press the ICE CREAM button.
7. Once done, take out the bowl from the Ninja CREAMi.
8. Serve and enjoy your delicious ice cream!

Vanilla Peanut Butter Ice Cream

Prep time: 10 minutes | Cook time: 10 minutes | Freeze time: 24 hours | Serves 4

- ½ cup peanut butter cups, chopped
- ¼ cup peanut butter chips
- ½ cup salted pretzels, crushed
- 1 cup whole milk
- ¾ cup heavy cream
- ⅓ cup granulated sugar

1. Add the ingredients to a blender. Mix well until smooth.
2. Pour the mixture into the Ninja CREAMi Pint and close it with the lid.
3. Place the pint into the freezer and freeze for 24 hours.
4. Once done, open the lid and set the pint into the outer bowl of the Ninja CREAMi. Put the Creamerizer Paddle into the outer bowl.
5. Lock the lid by rotating it clockwise.
6. Turn on the unit and press the ICE CREAM button.
7. Once done, take out the bowl from the Ninja CREAMi.
8. Serve and enjoy.

Cookies and Coconut Ice Cream

Prep time: 5 minutes | Freeze time: 24 hours | Serves 4

- 1 (14-ounce) can full-fat unsweetened coconut milk
- ½ cup organic sugar
- 1 teaspoon vanilla extract
- 4 chocolate sandwich cookies, crushed

1. In a medium bowl, whisk together the coconut milk, sugar, and vanilla until well combined and the sugar is dissolved.
2. Pour the base into a clean CREAMi Pint. Place the storage lid on the container and freeze for 24 hours.
3. Remove the pint from the freezer and take off the lid. Place the pint in the outer bowl of your Ninja® CREAMi™, install the Creamerizer™ Paddle in the outer bowl lid, and lock the lid assembly onto the outer bowl. Place the bowl assembly on the motor base, and twist the handle to the right to raise the platform and lock it in place. Select the Ice Cream function.
4. Once the machine has finished processing, remove the lid from the pint container. With a spoon, create a 1½-inch-wide hole that reaches the bottom of the pint. During this process, it is okay if your treat reaches above the Max Fill line. Add the crushed cookies to the hole in the pint, replace the lid, and select the Mix-In function.
5. Once the machine has finished processing, remove the ice cream from the pint. Serve immediately with desired toppings.

Triple-Chocolate Ice Cream

Prep time: 5 minutes | Cook time: 7-10 minutes | Freeze time: 24 hours | Serves 4

- 4 large egg yolks
- ⅓ cup granulated sugar
- 1 tablespoon unsweetened cocoa powder
- 1 tablespoon hot fudge sauce
- ¾ cup heavy (whipping) cream
- ½ cup whole milk
- 1 teaspoon vanilla extract
- ¼ cup white chocolate chips

1. Fill a large bowl with ice water and set it aside.
2. In a small saucepan, whisk together the egg yolks, sugar, and cocoa powder until the mixture is fully combined and the sugar is dissolved. Do not do this over heat.
3. Whisk in the hot fudge, heavy cream, milk, and vanilla.
4. Place the pan over medium heat. Cook, stirring constantly with a rubber spatula, until the temperature reaches 165°F to 175°F on an instant-read thermometer.
5. Remove the pan from the heat and pour the base through a fine-mesh strainer into a clean CREAMi Pint. Carefully place the container in the prepared ice water bath, making sure the water doesn't spill into the base.
6. Once the base has cooled, place the storage lid on the pint and freeze for 24 hours.
7. Remove the pint from the freezer and take off the lid. Place the pint in the outer bowl of your Ninja® CREAMi™, install the Creamerizer™ Paddle in the outer bowl lid, and lock the lid assembly onto the outer bowl. Place the bowl assembly on the motor base, and twist the handle to the right to raise the platform and lock it in place. Select the Ice Cream function.
8. Once the machine has finished processing, remove the lid from the pint container. With a spoon, create a 1½-inch-wide hole that reaches the bottom of the pint. During this process, it is okay if your treat reaches above the Max Fill line. Add the white chocolate chips to the hole in the pint, replace the lid, and select the Mix-In function.
9. Once the machine has finished processing, remove the ice cream from the pint. Serve immediately with desired toppings.

Pistachio Ice Cream

Prep time: 5 minutes | Cook time: 3 minutes | Serves 4

- 1 tablespoon cream cheese, softened
- ⅓ cup granulated sugar
- 1 teaspoon almond extract
- 1 cup whole milk
- ¾ cup heavy cream
- ¼ cup pistachios, shells removed and chopped

1. In a large microwave-safe bowl, add the cream cheese and microwave on High for about ten seconds.
2. Remove from the microwave and stir until smooth.
3. Add the sugar and almond extract and with a wire whisk, beat until the mixture looks like frosting.
4. Slowly add the milk and heavy cream and beat until well combined.
5. Transfer the mixture into an empty Ninja CREAMi pint container.
6. Cover the container with storage lid and freeze for 24 hours.
7. After 24 hours, remove the lid from container and arrange into the Outer Bowl of Ninja CREAMi.
8. Install the Creamerizer Paddle onto the lid of Outer Bowl.
9. Then rotate the lid clockwise to lock.
10. Press Power button to turn on the unit.
11. Then press Ice Cream button.
12. When the program is completed, with a spoon, create a 1½-inch wide hole in the center that reaches the bottom of the pint container.
13. Add the pistachios into the hole and press Mix-In button.
14. When the program is completed, turn the Outer Bowl and release it from the machine.
15. Transfer the ice cream into serving bowls and serve immediately.

Jelly & Peanut Butter Ice Cream

Prep time: 5 minutes | Cook time: 5 minutes | Serves 4

- 3 tablespoons granulated sugar
- 4 large egg yolks
- 1 cup whole milk
- ⅓ cup heavy cream
- ¼ cup smooth peanut butter
- 3 tablespoons grape jelly
- ¼ cup honey roasted peanuts, chopped

1. In a small saucepan, add the sugar and egg yolks and beat until sugar is dissolved.
2. Add the milk, heavy cream, peanut butter, and grape jelly to the saucepan and stir to combine.
3. Place saucepan over medium heat and cook until temperature reaches cook until temperature reaches to 165 ~175° F, stirring continuously with a rubber spatula.
4. Remove from the heat and through a fine-mesh strainer, strain the mixture into an empty Ninja CREAMi pint container.
5. Place the container into ice bath to cool.
6. After cooling, cover the container with storage lid and freeze for 24 hours.
7. After 24 hours, remove the lid from container and arrange into the Outer Bowl of Ninja CREAMi.
8. Install the Creamerizer Paddle onto the lid of Outer Bowl.
9. Then rotate the lid clockwise to lock.
10. Press Power button to turn on the unit.
11. Then press ICE CREAM button.
12. When the program is completed, with a spoon, create a 1½-inch wide hole in the center that reaches the bottom of the pint container.
13. Add the peanuts into the hole and press Mix-In button.
14. When the program is completed, turn the Outer Bowl and release it from the machine.
15. Transfer the ice cream into serving bowls and serve immediately.

Vanilla Ice Cream With Chocolate Chips

Prep time: 5 minutes | Cook time: 5 minutes | Serves 4

- 1 tablespoon cream cheese, softened
- ⅓ cup granulated sugar
- 1 teaspoon vanilla extract
- ¾ cup heavy cream
- 1 cup whole milk
- ¼ cup mini chocolate chips, for mix-in

1. Microwave the cream cheese for 10 seconds in a large microwave-safe bowl. With a rubber spatula, blend in the sugar and vanilla extract until the mixture resembles frosting, about 60 seconds.
2. Slowly whisk in the heavy cream and milk until smooth and the sugar has dissolved.
3. Pour the base into an empty CREAMi Pint. Place the storage lid on the Pint and freeze for 24 hours.
4. Remove the Pint from the freezer and remove the lid from the Pint. Place the Pint in the outer bowl, install the Creamerizer Paddle onto the outer bowl lid, and lock the lid assembly on the outer bowl. Select ICE CREAM.
5. With a spoon, create a 1½-inch wide hole that reaches the bottom of the Pint. During this process, it's okay for your treat to press above the max fill line. Add chocolate chips to the hole in the Pint and process again using the MIX-IN program.
6. When processing is complete, remove the ice cream from the Pint.

Mint Chocolate Chip Ice Cream

Prep time: 5 minutes | Cook time: 5 minutes | Freeze time: 24 hours | Serves 4

- 1 tablespoon cream cheese, softened
- ⅓ cup granulated sugar
- 1 teaspoon vanilla extract
- ¾ cup heavy cream
- 1 cup whole milk
- 1 teaspoon mint extract
- Green food coloring (optional)
- ¼ cup mini chocolate chips, for mix-in

1. Microwave the cream cheese for 10 seconds in a large microwave-safe bowl. Combine with the sugar and mint extract in a mixing bowl using a whisk or rubber spatula for about 60 seconds or until the mixture resembles frosting.
2. Slowly whisk in the heavy cream, milk, and optional food coloring until thoroughly mixed and the sugar has dissolved.
3. Pour the base into an empty CREAMi Pint. Place the storage lid on the Pint and freeze for 24 hours.
4. Remove the Pint from the freezer and remove its lid. Place the Pint in the outer bowl, install the Creamerizer Paddle onto the outer bowl lid, and lock the lid assembly on the outer bowl.

Place the bowl assembly on the motor base, twist the handle to raise the platform, and lock it in place.
5. Select ICE CREAM.
6. With a spoon, create a 1½-inch wide hole that reaches the bottom of the Pint. During this process, it's okay for your treat to press above the max fill line. Add the chocolate chips to the hole and process again using the MIX-IN program.
7. When processing is complete, remove the ice cream from the Pint.

Rum Raisin Ice Cream

Prep time: 23 minutes | Cook time: 23 minutes | Freeze time: 24 hours | Serves 4

- 3 large egg yolks
- ¼ cup dark brown sugar (or coconut sugar)
- 1 tablespoon light corn syrup
- ½ cup heavy cream
- 1 cup whole milk
- 1 teaspoon rum extract
- ⅓ cup raisins
- ¼ cup dark or spiced rum

1. In a small saucepan, combine the egg yolks, sugar, and corn syrup. Whisk until everything is well mixed and the sugar has dissolved. Whisk together the heavy cream and milk until smooth.
2. Stir the mixture frequently with a whisk or a rubber spatula in a saucepan over medium-low heat. Using an instant-read thermometer, cook until the temperature hits 165°F–175°F.
3. Remove the base from heat, stir in the rum extract, then pour through a fine-mesh strainer into an empty CREAMi Pint. Place into an ice bath. Once cooled, place the storage lid on the Pint and freeze for 24 hours.
4. While the base is cooling, prepare the mix-in. Add the raisins and rum to a small bowl and microwave for 1 minute. Let cool, then drain the remaining rum. Cover and set aside.
5. Remove the Pint from the freezer and remove its lid. Place the Pint in the outer bowl, install the Creamerizer Paddle onto the outer bowl lid, and lock the lid assembly on the outer bowl. Select ICE CREAM.
6. With a spoon, create a 1½-inch wide hole that reaches the bottom of the Pint. Add the mixed raisins to the hole and process again using the MIX-IN program.
7. When processing is complete, remove the ice cream from the Pint.

Chapter 4
Ice Cream Recipes

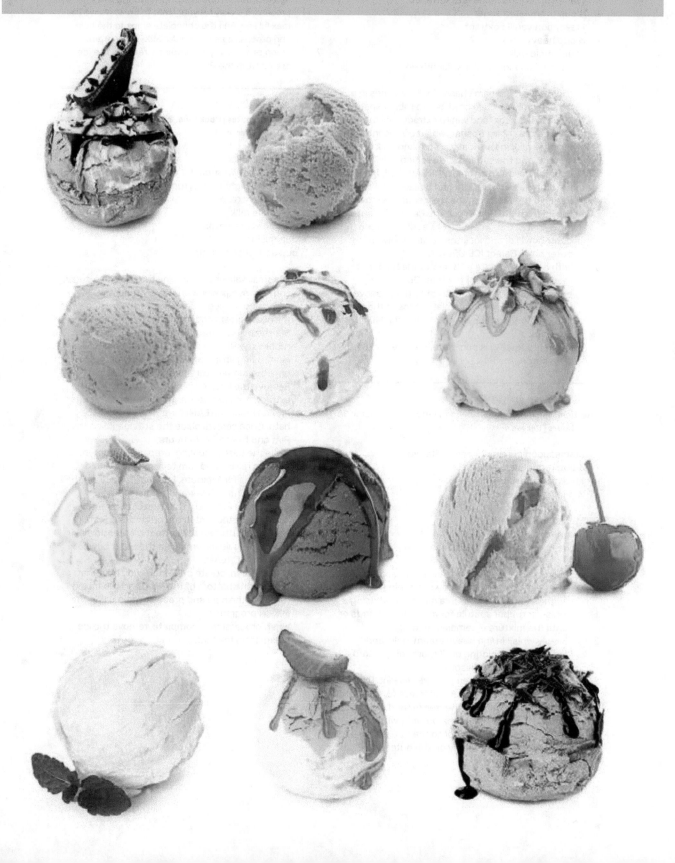

Low-sugar Vanilla Ice Cream

Prep time: 5 minutes | Cook time: 5 minutes | Serves 4

- 1¾ cup fat-free half-and-half
- ¼ cup stevia cane sugar blend
- 1 teaspoon vanilla extract

1. In a medium bowl, whisk the half-and-half, sugar, and vanilla together until everything is combined and the sugar is dissolved. The mixture will be foamy. Let it sit for 5 minutes or until the foam subsides.
2. Pour the base into a clean CREAMi Pint. Place the storage lid on the container and freeze for 24 hours.
3. Remove the CREAMi Pint from the freezer and take off the lid. Place the pint in the outer bowl of your Ninja CREAMi, install the Creamerizer Paddle in the outer bowl lid, and lock the lid assembly onto the outer bowl. Place the bowl assembly on the motor base, and twist the handle to the right to raise the platform and lock it in place. Select the Lite Ice Cream function.
4. Once the machine has finished processing, remove the ice cream from the pint. Serve immediately.

Coconut Ice-cream Of Togetherness

Prep Time: 10 minutes | Cook time: 24 hours 25 minutes | Serves 2

- ½ cup sweetened flaked coconut
- ¾ cup heavy cream
- 7 ounces cream of coconut
- ½ cup milk

1. In a food processor or blender, combine the milk and coconut cream and thoroughly mix.
2. Combine the heavy cream and flaked coconut in a mixing bowl, and then add to the milk-cream mixture. Combine well.
3. Pour the mixture into an empty ninja CREAMi Pint container and freeze for 24 hours.
4. After 24 hours, remove the Pint from the freezer. Remove the lid.
5. Place the Ninja CREAMi Pint into the outer bowl. Next, place the outer bowl with the Pint into the ninja CREAMi machine and turn until the outer bowl locks into place. Then, push the ICE CREAM button.
6. Once the ICE CREAM function has ended, turn the outer bowl and release it from the ninja CREAMi machine.

Lavender Cookies And Cream Delight

Prep Time: 10 minutes | Cook time: 24 hours | Serves 2

- ½ cup heavy cream
- ½ tablespoon dried lavender
- ½ cup whole milk
- ¼ cup sweetened condensed milk
- 2 drops purple food coloring
- ¼ cup crushed chocolate wafer cookies

1. Whisk together the heavy cream, lavender, and salt in a medium saucepan.
2. Steep the mixture for 10 minutes over low heat, stirring every 2 minutes to prevent bubbling.
3. Using a fine-mesh strainer, drain the lavender from the heavy cream into a large mixing basin. Discard the lavender.
4. Combine the milk, sweetened condensed milk, and purple food coloring in a large mixing bowl. Whisk until the mixture is completely smooth.
5. Pour the base into an empty CREAMi Pint. Place the Pint into an ice bath. Once cooled, place the storage lid on the Pint and freeze for 24 hours.
6. Remove the Pint from the freezer and remove its lid. Place Pint in outer bowl, install Creamerizer Paddle in outer bowl lid, and lock the lid assembly onto the outer bowl. Select ICE CREAM.
7. When the process is done, create a 1 Vfe-inch wide hole that reaches the bottom of the Pint with a spoon. It's okay if your treat exceeds the max fill line. Add crushed wafer cookies to the hole and process again using the MIX-IN program.
8. When processing is complete, remove ice cream from Pint and serve immediately, topped with extra crumbled wafers if desired.

Mellowness Walnut Ice Cream

Prep time: 10 minutes | Cook time: 10 minutes | Freeze time: 24 hours | Serves 4

- 1 cup whole milk
- 3 tablespoons walnut paste, smooth
- 1 tablespoon heavy whipped cream
- 1 teaspoon vanilla extract

1. In a large bowl, merge together all the ingredients until combined.
2. Move the mixture into an empty Ninja CREAMI pint.
3. Fasten the lid of the pint and freeze for 24 hours.
4. After 24 hours, open the pint, fix it into the outer bowl of Ninja CREAMi along with the 'Creamerizer paddle'.
5. Fasten the lid, turn on the 'Power Button', and select the 'ICE CREAM' function.
6. Dish out the ice cream from the pint and serve chilled.

Carrot Ice Cream

Prep time: 5 minutes | Cook time: 1 minutes | Serves 2

- 1 cup heavy cream
- ½ cup carrot juice
- ⅓ cup light brown sugar
- 2 tablespoons cream cheese frosting
- 1 teaspoon vanilla extract
- 1 teaspoon ground cinnamon

1. In a bowl, add all ingredients and beat until well combined.
2. Transfer the mixture into an empty Ninja CREAMi pint container.
3. Cover the container with the storage lid and freeze for 24 hours
4. After 24 hours, remove the lid from container and arrange into the outer bowl of Ninja CREAMi.
5. Install the "Creamerizer Paddle" onto the lid of outer bowl.
6. Then rotate the lid clockwise to lock.
7. Press "Power" button to turn on the unit.
8. Then press "ICE CREAM" button.
9. When the program is completed, turn the outer bowl and release it from the machine.
10. Transfer the ice cream into serving bowls and serve immediately.

The Golden Rocky Road

Prep Time: 10 minutes | Cook time: 24 hours | Serves 2

- ½ cup whole milk
- ¼ cup frozen cauliflower florets, thawed
- ¼ cup dark brown sugar
- 1 tablespoon dark cocoa powder
- ½ teaspoon chocolate extract
- ¼ cup heavy cream
- 1 tablespoon sliced almonds
- 1 tablespoon mini chocolate chip
- 1 tablespoon mini marshmallow, mix in

1. In a blender pitcher, combine the milk, cauliflower, brown sugar, cocoa powder, and chocolate essence. Blend on high for about 60 seconds, or until the mixture is totally smooth.
2. Pour the base into an empty CREAMi Pint. Add heavy cream and stir until well combined. Place the storage lid on the Pint and freeze for 24 hours.
3. Remove the Pint from the freezer and remove the lid from the Pint. Place Pint in outer bowl, install Creamerizer Paddle onto outer bowl lid and lock the lid assembly on the outer bowl. Select ICE CREAM.
4. With a spoon, create a life-inch wide hole that reaches the bottom of the Pint. Add the sliced almonds, chocolate chips, and marshmallows to the hole and process using the MIX-IN program.
5. When processing is complete, remove the ice cream from the Pint and serve immediately.

PER SERVING

Calories: 217 | Fat:31g | Carbohydrates:18g | Protein:5g

Aroma Coconut Ice Cream

Prep time: 10 minutes | Cook time: 10 minutes | Freeze time: 24 hours | Serves 4

- 2 tablespoons coconut, shredded
- 1 cup full-fat unsweetened coconut milk
- 2 tablespoon whipped cream
- ⅓ cup sugar, granulated

1. In a saucepan, merge together all the ingredients and simmer for 10 minutes.
2. Eliminate from heat and blitz the mixture after it is cooled down.
3. Move the mixture into an empty Ninja CREAMi pint.
4. Fasten the lid of the pint and freeze for 24 hours.
5. After 24 hours, open the pint, fix it into the outer bowl of Ninja CREAMi along with the 'Creamerizer paddle'.
6. Fasten the lid, turn on the 'Power Button', and select the 'ICE CREAM' function.
7. Dish out the ice cream from the pint and serve chilled.

Cinnamon Red Hot Ice Cream

Prep time: 10 minutes | Cook time: 10 minutes | Freeze time: 24 hours | Serves 5

- 2 cups heavy whipping cream, divided
- 1 egg yolk
- 1 cup half-and-half
- ½ cup Red Hot candies

1. In a mixing bowl, whisk together 1 cup of cream and the egg yolks until smooth.
2. In another large bowl, combine the half-and-half, 1 cup cream, and Red Hot candies. Whisk with a wooden spoon until the candies dissolve, about 5 to 10 minutes.
3. Pour the cream-egg mixture into the candy mixture and stir to incorporate.
4. Pour the mixture into an empty ninja CREAMi Pint container and freeze for 24 hours.
5. After 24 hours, remove the Pint from the freezer. Remove the lid.
6. Place the Ninja CREAMi Pint into the outer bowl. Place the outer bowl with the Pint in it into the ninja CREAMi machine and turn until the outer bowl locks into place. Push the ICE CREAM button.
7. Once the ICE CREAM function has ended, turn the outer bowl and release it from the ninja CREAMi machine.

Pumpkin Gingersnap Ice Cream

Prep time: 15 minutes | Cook time: 15 minutes | Freeze time: 24 hours | Serves 4

- 1 cup heavy whipping cream
- ½ tablespoon vanilla extract
- ½ teaspoon ground cinnamon
- ½ teaspoon ground ginger
- ½ cup solid-pack pumpkin
- 1 (7 ounces) can Eagle Brand sweetened condensed milk
- ½ cup crushed gingersnap cookies

1. In a large mixing bowl, beat the heavy whipping cream, vanilla extract, cinnamon, and ginger with an electric mixer on medium speed until stiff peaks form.
2. Combine the pumpkin and sweetened condensed milk in a mixing bowl.
3. Add the crushed gingersnap cookies to the pumpkin mixture and stir well.
4. Pour the mixture into an empty ninja CREAMi Pint container and freeze for 24 hours.
5. After 24 hours, remove the Pint from the freezer. Remove the lid.
6. Place the Ninja CREAMi Pint into the outer bowl. Place the outer bowl with the Pint in it into the ninja CREAMi machine and turn until the outer bowl locks into place. Push the ICE CREAM button.
7. Once the ICE CREAM function has ended, turn the outer bowl and release it from the ninja CREAMi machine.

Canary Pear Ice Cream

Prep time: 15 minutes | **Cook time:** 15 minutes | **Freeze time:** 24 hours | **Serves 4**

- 1 (14-ounce) can full-fat unsweetened coconut milk
- 3 medium pears, peeled, cored and cut into 1-inch pieces
- ½ cup sugar, granulated

1. In a saucepan, merge together all the ingredients and stir well.
2. Thoroughly boil and switch the heat to low, so that it simmers for 10 minutes.
3. Eliminate from the heat and blitz the mixture after it is cooled down.
4. Move the mixture into an empty Ninja CREAMI pint.
5. Fasten the lid of the pint and freeze for 24 hours.
6. After 24 hours, open the pint, fix it into the outer bowl of Ninja CREAMi along with the 'Creamerizer paddle'.
7. Fasten the lid, turn on the 'Power Button', and select the 'ICE CREAM' function.
8. Dish out the ice cream from the pint and serve chilled.

Crunchy Cracker Ice Cream

Prep time: 15 minutes | **Cook time:** 35 minutes | **Freeze time:** 24 hours | **Serves 6**

- ½ cup Buncha Crunch
- ½ teaspoon vanilla extract
- 1½ cups heavy cream
- ¼ teaspoon xanthan gum
- ½ teaspoon salt
- ½ cup mini chocolate chips
- 1 tablespoon corn syrup
- 1½ cups whole milk
- 8 graham crackers, crushed
- ½ cup light brown sugar

1. In a bowl, merge the brown sugar with graham crackers, salt, and xanthan gum.
2. In a saucepan, cook the milk, cream, corn syrup, and sugar mixture until all lumps are dissolved.
3. Eliminate the pot from heat and fold in the vanilla extract, chocolate chips, and Buncha Crunch.
4. Move the mixture into an empty Ninja CREAMI pint after refrigerating for 6 hours.
5. Fasten the lid of the pint and freeze for 24 hours.
6. After 24 hours, open the pint, fix it into the outer bowl of Ninja CREAMi along with the 'Creamerizer paddle'.
7. Fasten the lid, turn on the 'Power Button', and select the 'ICE CREAM' function.
8. Dish out the ice cream from the pint and serve chilled.

Mint Cookie Ice Cream

Prep time: 5 minutes | **Cook time:** 5 minutes | **Serves 4**

- ¾ cup coconut cream
- ¼ cup monk fruit sweetener with Erythritol
- 2 tablespoons agave nectar
- ½ teaspoon mint extract
- 5-6 drops green food coloring
- 1 cup oat milk
- 3 chocolate sandwich cookies, quartered

1. In a large bowl, add the coconut cream and beat until smooth.
2. Add the sweetener, agave nectar, mint extract and food coloring and beat until sweetener is dissolved.
3. Add the oat milk and beat until well combined.
4. Transfer the mixture into an empty Ninja CREAMi pint container.
5. Cover the container with the storage lid and freeze for 24 hours.
6. After 24 hours, remove the lid from container and arrange into the outer bowl of Ninja CREAMi.
7. Install the "Creamerizer Paddle" onto the lid of outer bowl.
8. Then rotate the lid clockwise to lock.
9. Press "Power" button to turn on the unit.
10. Then press "LITE ICE CREAM" button.
11. When the program is completed, with a spoon, create a 1½-inch wide hole in the center that reaches the bottom of the pint container.
12. Add the cookie pieces into the hole and press "MIX-IN" button.
13. When the program is completed, turn the outer bowl and release it from the machine.
14. Transfer the ice cream into serving bowls and serve immediately.

Matcha Ice Cream

Prep time: 15 minutes | Cook time: 15 minutes | Freeze time: 24 hours | Serves 4

- 1 tablespoon cream cheese, softened
- ⅓ cup granulated sugar
- 2 tablespoons matcha powder
- 1 teaspoon vanilla extract
- 1 cup whole milk
- ¾ cup heavy cream

1. In a large microwave-safe bowl, add the cream cheese and microwave for on High for about ten seconds.
2. Remove from the microwave and stir until smooth.
3. Add the sugar, matcha powder and vanilla extract and with a wire whisk, beat until the mixture looks like frosting.
4. Slowly add the milk and heavy cream and beat until well combined.
5. Transfer the mixture into an empty Ninja CREAMi pint container.
6. Cover the container with storage lid and freeze for 24 hours.
7. After 24 hours, remove the lid from container and arrange into the Outer Bowl of Ninja CREAMi.
8. Install the Creamerizer Paddle onto the lid of Outer Bowl.
9. Then rotate the lid clockwise to lock.
10. Press Power button to turn on the unit.
11. Then press Ice Cream button.
12. When the program is completed, turn the Outer Bowl and release it from the machine.
13. Transfer the ice cream into serving bowls and serve immediately.

Vanilla Corn Ice Cream

Prep time: 10 minutes | Cook time: 5 minutes | Freeze time: 24 hours | Serves 1

- 1 cup cold milk
- ¼ tablespoon corn flour
- ¼ cup fresh cream
- ¼ cup sugar
- ½ teaspoon vanilla essence

1. In a small bowl, whisk together the corn flour and milk to make a smooth paste. If you don't use cold milk, you'll end up with lumps. Combine all of the ingredients in a mixing bowl and set aside. Mix in the remaining milk, vanilla extract, and sugar.
1. Pour the mixture into an empty ninja CREAMi Pint container and freeze for 24 hours.
2. After 24 hours, remove the Pint from the freezer. Remove the lid.
3. Place the Ninja CREAMi Pint into the outer bowl. Place the outer bowl with the Pint in it into the ninja CREAMi machine and turn until the outer bowl locks into place. Push the ICE CREAM button. During the ICE CREAM function, the ice cream will mix together and become very creamy.
4. Once the ICE CREAM function has ended, turn the outer bowl and release it from the ninja CREAMi machine.

Earl Grey Tea Ice Cream

Prep time: 15 minutes | Cook time: 15 minutes | Freeze time: 24 hours | Serves 4

- 1 cup heavy cream
- 1 cup whole milk
- 5 tablespoons monk fruit sweetener
- 3 Earl Grey tea bags

1. In a medium saucepan, add cream and milk and stir to combine.
2. Place saucepan over medium heat and cook until for bout two-three minutes or until steam is rising.
3. Stir in the monk fruit sweetener and reduce the heat to very low.
4. Add teabags and cover the saucepan for about 20 minutes.
5. Discard the tea bags and remove saucepan from heat.
6. Transfer the mixture into an empty Ninja CREAMi pint container and place into an ice bath to cool.
7. After cooling, cover the container with storage lid and freeze for 24 hours.
8. After 24 hours, remove the lid from container and arrange into the Outer Bowl of Ninja CREAMi.
9. Install the Creamerizer Paddle onto the lid of Outer Bowl.
10. Then rotate the lid clockwise to lock.
11. Press Power button to turn on the unit.
12. Then press Ice Cream button.
13. When the program is completed, turn the Outer Bowl and release it from the machine.
14. Transfer the ice cream into serving bowls and serve immediately.

Strawberry-carrot Ice Cream

Prep time: 5 minutes | Cook time: 5 minutes | Serves 4

- 1 cup frozen carrot slices, thawed
- ½ cup trimmed and quartered fresh strawberries
- 1 tablespoon cream cheese, at room temperature
- ⅓ cup granulated sugar
- 1 teaspoon strawberry extract
- ½ cup whole milk
- 5 drops red food coloring
- ½ cup heavy (whipping) cream

1. Combine the carrots, strawberries, cream cheese, sugar, strawberry extract, milk, and food coloring in a blender. Blend on high until smooth.
2. Pour the base into a clean CREAMi Pint. Whisk in the heavy cream until combined. Place the storage lid on the container and freeze for 24 hours.
3. Remove the CREAMi Pint from the freezer and take off the lid. Place the pint in the outer bowl of your Ninja CREAMi, install the Creamerizer Paddle in the outer bowl lid, and lock the lid assembly onto the outer bowl. Place the bowl assembly on the motor base, and twist the handle to the right to raise the platform and lock it in place. Select the Ice Cream function.
4. Once the machine has finished processing, remove the ice cream from the pint. Serve immediately with desired toppings.

Fruity Extract Ice Cream

Prep time: 5 minutes | Cook time: 5 minutes | Serves 4

- 1 cup whole milk
- ¾ cup heavy cream
- 2 tablespoons monk fruit sweetener with Erythritol
- 2 tablespoons agave nectar
- ½ teaspoon raspberry extract
- ½ teaspoon vanilla extract
- ¼ teaspoon lemon extract
- 5-6 drops blue food coloring

1. In a bowl, add all ingredients and eat until well combined.
2. Transfer the mixture into an empty Ninja CREAMi pint container.
3. Cover the container with storage lid and freeze for 24 hours.
4. After 24 hours, remove the lid from container and arrange into the Outer Bowl of Ninja CREAMi.
5. Install the Creamerizer Paddle onto the lid of outer bowl.
6. Then rotate the lid clockwise to lock.
7. Press Power button to turn on the unit.
8. Then press Ice Cream button.
9. When the program is completed, turn the Outer Bowl and release it from the machine.
10. Transfer the ice cream into serving bowls and serve immediately.

Kale'd By Chocolate Ice Cream

Prep time: 5 minutes | Cook time: 5 minutes | Serves 4

- 1 cup frozen kale
- 1 tablespoon cream cheese, at room temperature
- ⅓ cup granulated sugar
- 3 tablespoons dark unsweetened cocoa powder
- ¾ cup whole milk
- ¾ cup heavy (whipping) cream

1. Combine the frozen kale, cream cheese, sugar, cocoa powder, and milk in a blender. Blend on high until smooth.
2. Pour the base into a clean CREAMi Pint. Whisk in the heavy cream until combined. Place the storage lid on the container and freeze for 24 hours.
3. Remove the CREAMi Pint from the freezer and take off the lid. Place the pint in the outer bowl of your Ninja CREAMi, install the Creamerizer Paddle in outer bowl lid, and lock the lid assembly onto the outer bowl. Place the bowl assembly on the motor base, and twist the handle to the right to raise the platform and lock it in place. Select the Ice Cream function.
4. Once the machine has finished processing, remove the ice cream from the pint. Serve immediately with desired toppings.

Chapter 5
Gelato Recipes

Big Blueberry Chocolate Gelato

Prep time: 5 minutes | Cook time: 2 hours 35 minutes | Serves 4-6

- 1/2 cup heavy cream
- 2 cups milk
- 3/4 cup sugar
- 1 teaspoon vanilla extract
- 1 cup blueberries
- ½ cup finely chopped semi-sweet

1. Refer to note at the beginning of the chapter about freezing bowl.
2. Puree the bananas in a food processor or blender.
3. Place the milk and cream in a bowl, and mix them together until well combined. Use a whisk to mix in the sugar. Continue to whisk for about 4 minutes until the sugar dissolves. Then mix in the vanilla extract and banana puree.
4. Pour the ingredients into your ice cream maker, and let it churn for 25 minutes. About 5 minutes before the ice cream is done churning add the chocolate to your ice cream maker.
5. Put the gelato in an airtight container and place in the freezer for up to 2 hours, until desired consistency is reached.

Pulsating Pomegranate Mint Frozen Yogurt

Prep time: 5 minutes | Cook time: 2 hours 35 minutes | Makes 1 quart

- 1 quart container full-fat plain yogurt
- ¼ teaspoon salt
- 1 cup sugar
- 1 tablespoon mint extract
- 1 cup 100% pomegranate juice
- 1/2 cup semi-sweet chocolate chips

1. Refer to note at the beginning of the chapter about freezing bowl.
2. Place the yogurt in a bowl. Use a whisk to mix in the sugar and salt. Continue to whisk for about 4 minutes until the sugar dissolves. Then mix in the mint extract, and pomegranate juice.
3. Pour the ingredients into your ice cream maker, and let it churn for 25 minutes. About 5 minutes before the ice cream is done churning add the chocolate chips to your ice cream maker.
4. Put the frozen yogurt in an airtight container and place in the freezer for at least 2 hours, until desired consistency is reached.

Tropical Coconut Rum And Coke Gelato

Prep time: 5 minutes | Cook time: 2 hours 50 minutes | Serves 4-6

- 1/2 cup heavy cream
- 2 cups milk
- 3/4 cup sugar
- 1 teaspoon vanilla extract
- 3 tablespoons rum
- ¼ cup shaved coconut
- 3 cups coca cola (2, 12 ounce cans)

1. Pour the coke into a large skillet, and heat it on high heat until it comes to a boil. Allow the coke to cook for about another 15 or 20 minutes, until the coke reduces down to 1 cup of liquid. Let the liquid cool.
2. Place the milk and cream in a bowl, and mix them together until well combined. Use a whisk to mix in the sugar. Continue to whisk for about 4 minutes until the sugar dissolves. Then mix in the vanilla extract, coke reduction, coconut chips and rum.
3. Pour the ingredients into your ice cream maker, and let it churn for 25 minutes.
4. Put the gelato in an airtight container and place in the freezer for up to 2 hours, until desired consistency is reached.

Kaffir Lime Gelato

Prep time: 5 minutes | Cook time: 5 minutes | Serves 2-4

- 9 frozen bananas, peeled
- 1 cup coconut cream
- 1 teaspoon lime juice
- 2 tablespoons lime zest
- 3 kaffir lime leaves, finely chopped

1. Place a large mixing bowl under the Yonanas chute and push the bananas through.
2. Fold in coconut cream, lime juice, and kaffir lime leaves.
3. Spoon into individual bowls and top with a sprinkle of lime zest.
4. Freeze leftovers in an airtight container.

Kickin' Kiwi Lime Ice Cream

Prep time: 5 minutes | Cook time: 2 hours 50 minutes | Serves 6

- 2 cups heavy cream
- 1 cup milk
- 3/4 cup sugar
- 1/2 teaspoon vanilla extract
- ½ teaspoon salt
- 1 kiwi, peeled
- Juice of one and a half limes

1. Refer to note at the beginning of the chapter about freezing bowl.
2. Puree the kiwi in a food processor or blender.
3. Place the milk and cream in a bowl, and mix them together until well combined. Use a whisk to mix in the sugar and salt. Continue to whisk for about 4 minutes until the sugar and salt dissolves. Then mix in the vanilla extract, lime juice, and kiwi puree.
4. Pour the ingredients into your ice cream maker, and let it churn for 25 minutes.
5. Put the ice cream in an airtight container and place in the freezer for around 2 hours. Allow the ice cream to thaw for 15 minutes before serving.

Carrot Gelato

Prep time: 10 minutes | Cook time: 8 minutes | Freeze time: 24 hours | Serves 4

- 3 large egg yolks
- ⅓ cup coconut sugar
- 1 tablespoon brown rice syrup
- ½ cup heavy cream
- 1 cup unsweetened almond milk
- ½ cup carrot purée
- ½ teaspoon ground cinnamon
- ¼ teaspoon ground nutmeg
- ¼ teaspoon ground ginger
- ¼ teaspoon ground cloves
- ¾ teaspoon vanilla extract

1. In a small saucepan, add the egg yolks, coconut sugar and brown rice syrup and beat until well combined.
2. Add the heavy cream, almond milk, carrot purée and spices and beat until well combined.
3. Place the saucepan over medium heat and cook for about 2-3 minutes, stirring continuously.
4. Remove from the heat and stir in the vanilla extract.
5. Through a fine-mesh strainer, strain the mixture into an empty Ninja CREAMi pint container.
6. Place the container into an ice bath to cool.
7. After cooling, cover the container with the storage lid and freeze for 24 hours.
8. After 24 hours, remove the lid from container and arrange into the outer bowl of Ninja CREAMi.
9. Install the "Creamerizer Paddle" onto the lid of outer bowl.
10. Then rotate the lid clockwise to lock.
11. Press "Power" button to turn on the unit.
12. Then press "GELATO" button.
13. When the program is completed, turn the outer bowl and release it from the machine.
14. Transfer the gelato into bowls and serve immediately.

Blueberry & Crackers Gelato

Prep time: 10 minutes | Cook time: 3 minutes | Serves 4

- 4 large egg yolks
- 3 tablespoons granulated sugar
- 3 tablespoons wild blueberry preserves
- 1 teaspoon vanilla extract
- 1 cup whole milk
- ⅓ cup heavy cream
- ¼ cup cream cheese, softened
- 3-6 drops purple food coloring
- 2 large graham crackers, broken in 1-inch pieces

1. In a small saucepan, add the egg yolks, sugar, blueberry preserves and vanilla extract and beat until well combined.
2. Add the milk, heavy cream, cream cheese and food coloring and beat until well combined.
3. Place the saucepan over medium heat and cook for about 2-3 minutes, stirring continuously.
4. Remove from the heat and through a fine-mesh strainer, strain the mixture into an empty Ninja CREAMi pint container.
5. Place the container into an ice bath to cool.
6. After cooling, cover the container with the storage lid and freeze for 24 hours.
7. After 24 hours, remove the lid from container and arrange into the outer bowl of Ninja CREAMi.
8. Install the "Creamerizer Paddle" onto the lid of outer bowl.
9. Then rotate the lid clockwise to lock.
10. Press "Power" button to turn on the unit.
11. Then press "GELATO" button.
12. When the program is completed, with a spoon, create a 1½-inch wide hole in the center that reaches the bottom of the pint container.
13. Add the graham crackers into the hole and press "MIX-IN" button.
14. When the program is completed, turn the outer bowl and release it from the machine.
15. Transfer the gelato into serving bowls and serve immediately.

Pecan Gelato

Prep time: 10 minutes | Cook time: 8 minutes | Freeze time: 24 hours |Serves 4

- 4 large egg yolks
- 5 tablespoons granulated sugar
- 1 tablespoon light corn syrup
- 1 cup heavy cream
- ⅓ cup whole milk
- 1 teaspoon butter flavor extract
- ⅓ cup pecans, chopped

1. In a small saucepan, add the egg yolks, sugar and corn syrup and beat until well combined.
2. Add the heavy cream, milk and butter flavor extract and beat until well combined.
3. Place the saucepan over medium heat and cook for about 2-3 minutes, stirring continuously.
4. Remove from the heat and through a fine-mesh strainer, strain the mixture into an empty Ninja CREAMi pint container.
5. Place the container into an ice bath to cool.
6. After cooling, cover the container with the storage lid and freeze for 24 hours.
7. After 24 hours, remove the lid from container and arrange into the outer bowl of Ninja CREAMi.
8. Install the "Creamerizer Paddle" onto the lid of outer bowl.
9. Then rotate the lid clockwise to lock.
10. Press "Power" button to turn on the unit.
11. Then press "GELATO" button.
12. When the program is completed, with a spoon, create a 1½-inch wide hole in the center that reaches the bottom of the pint container.
13. Add the pecans into the hole and press "MIX-IN" button.
14. When the program is completed, turn the outer bowl and release it from the machine.
15. Transfer the gelato into bowls and serve immediately.

Butternut Squash Gelato

Prep time: 10 minutes | Cook time: 10 minutes | Freeze time: 24 hours |Serves 4

- 1¾ cups milk
- ½ cup cooked butternut squash
- ¼ cup granulated sugar
- ½ teaspoon ground cinnamon
- ¼ teaspoon ground allspice
- Pinch of salt

1. In a small saucepan, add all ingredients and beat until well combined.
2. Place the saucepan over medium heat and cook for about 5 minutes, stirring continuously.
3. Remove from the heat and transfer the mixture into an empty Ninja CREAMi pint container.
4. Place the container into an ice bath to cool.
5. After cooling, cover the container with the storage lid and freeze for 24 hours.
6. After 24 hours, remove the lid from container and arrange into the outer bowl of Ninja CREAMi.
7. Install the "Creamerizer Paddle" onto the lid of outer bowl.
8. Then rotate the lid clockwise to lock.
9. Press "Power" button to turn on the unit.
10. Then press "GELATO" button.
11. When the program is completed, turn the outer bowl and release it from the machine.
12. Transfer the gelato into bowls and serve immediately.

Blueberry Gelato

Prep time: 10 minutes | Cook time: 8 minutes | Freeze time: 24 hours | Serves 4

- 4 large egg yolks
- 3 tablespoons granulated sugar
- 3 tablespoons wild blueberry preserves
- 1 teaspoon vanilla extract
- 1 cup whole milk
- ⅓ cup heavy cream
- ¼ cup cream cheese, softened
- 3-6 drops purple food coloring
- 2 large graham crackers, broken in 1-inch pieces

1. In a small saucepan, add the egg yolks, sugar, blueberry preserves and vanilla extract and beat until well combined.
2. Add the milk, heavy cream, cream cheese and food coloring and beat until well combined.
3. Place the saucepan over medium heat and cook for about 2-3 minutes, stirring continuously.
4. Remove from the heat and through a fine-mesh strainer, strain the mixture into an empty Ninja CREAMi pint container.
5. Place the container into an ice bath to cool.
6. After cooling, cover the container with the storage lid and freeze for 24 hours.
7. After 24 hours, remove the lid from container and arrange into the outer bowl of Ninja CREAMi.
8. Install the "Creamerizer Paddle" onto the lid of outer bowl.
9. Then rotate the lid clockwise to lock.
10. Press "Power" button to turn on the unit.
11. Then press "GELATO" button.
12. When the program is completed, with a spoon, create a 1½-inch wide hole in the center that reaches the bottom of the pint container.
13. Add the graham crackers into the hole and press "MIX-IN" button.
14. When the program is completed, turn the outer bowl and release it from the machine.
15. Transfer the gelato into bowls and serve immediately.

Chocolate Hazelnut Gelato

Prep time: 10 minutes | Cook time: 8 minutes | Freeze time: 24 hours | Serves 4

- 3 large egg yolks
- ⅓ cup hazelnut spread
- ¼ cup granulated sugar
- 2 teaspoon cocoa powder
- 1 tablespoon light corn syrup
- 1 cup whole milk
- ½ cup heavy cream
- 1 teaspoon vanilla extract

1. In a small saucepan, add the egg yolks, hazelnut spread, sugar, cocoa powder and corn syrup and beat until well combined.
2. Add the milk, heavy cream and vanilla extract and beat until well combined.
3. Place the saucepan over medium heat and cook for about 2-3 minutes, stirring continuously.
4. Remove from the heat and through a fine-mesh strainer, strain the mixture into an empty Ninja CREAMi pint container.
5. Place the container into an ice bath to cool.
6. After cooling, cover the container with the storage lid and freeze for 24 hours.
7. After 24 hours, remove the lid from container and arrange into the outer bowl of Ninja CREAMi.
8. Install the "Creamerizer Paddle" onto the lid of outer bowl.
9. Then rotate the lid clockwise to lock.
10. Press "Power" button to turn on the unit.
11. Then press "GELATO" button.
12. When the program is completed, turn the outer bowl and release it from the machine.
13. Transfer the gelato into bowls and serve immediately.

Oatmeal Gelato

Prep time: 1 hour | Cook time: 24 hours | Serves 4

- 2 oz. instant oatmeal
- 1 cup hot water
- 1 tablespoon heavy cream powder
- 2 tablespoons yogurt

1. Add the oatmeal to a bowl.
2. Cover with hot water.
3. Let sit for 15 minutes.
4. Transfer oatmeal to your Ninja Creami pint container.
5. Stir in the rest of the ingredients.
6. Freeze for 24 hours.
7. Place in the machine.
8. Choose the Gelato function.

Triple Chocolate Gelato

Prep time: 10 minutes | Cook time: 8 minutes | Freeze time: 24 hours |Serves 4

- 4 large egg yolks
- ⅓ cup dark brown sugar
- 1 tablespoon dark cocoa powder
- 1 tablespoon chocolate fudge topping
- ¾ cup heavy cream
- ¾ cup whole milk
- 2-3 tablespoons chocolate chunks, chopped

1. In a small saucepan, add the egg yolks, sugar, cocoa powder and chocolate fudge and beat until well combined.
2. Add the heavy cream and milk and beat until well combined.
3. Place the saucepan over medium heat and cook for about 2-3 minutes, stirring continuously.
4. Remove from the heat and stir in chocolate chunks until melted completely.
5. Through a fine-mesh strainer, strain the mixture into an empty Ninja CREAMi pint container.
6. Place the container into an ice bath to cool.
7. After cooling, cover the container with the storage lid and freeze for 24 hours.
8. After 24 hours, remove the lid from container and arrange into the outer bowl of Ninja CREAMi.
9. Install the "Creamerizer Paddle" onto the lid of outer bowl.
10. Then rotate the lid clockwise to lock.
11. Press "Power" button to turn on the unit.
12. Then press "GELATO" button.
13. When the program is completed, turn the outer bowl and release it from the machine.
14. Transfer the gelato into bowls and serve immediately.

Vanilla Bean Gelato

Prep time: 5 minutes | Cook time: 3 minutes | Serves 4

- 4 large egg yolks
- 1 tablespoon light corn syrup
- ¼ cup plus 1 tablespoon granulated sugar
- ⅓ cup whole milk
- 1 cup heavy (whipping) cream
- 1 whole vanilla bean, split in half lengthwise and scraped

1. Fill a large bowl with ice water and set it aside.
2. In a small saucepan, whisk together the egg yolks, corn syrup, and sugar until everything is fully combined and the sugar is dissolved. Do not do this over heat.
3. Whisk in the milk, heavy cream, and vanilla bean scrapings (discard the pod).
4. Place the pan over medium heat. Cook, stirring constantly with a rubber spatula, until the temperature reaches 165°F to 175°F on an instant-read thermometer.
5. Remove the pan from the heat and pour the base through a fine-mesh strainer into a clean CREAMi Pint. Carefully place the container in the prepared ice water bath, making sure the water doesn't spill into the base.
6. Once the base has cooled, place the storage lid on the pint and freeze for 24 hours.
7. Remove the pint from the freezer and take off the lid. Place the pint in the outer bowl of your Ninja CREAMi, install the Creamerizer Paddle in the outer bowl lid, and lock the lid assembly onto the outer bowl. Place the bowl assembly on the motor base, and twist the handle to the right to raise the platform and lock it in place. Select the Gelato function.
8. Once the machine has finished processing, remove the gelato from the pint. Serve immediately with desired toppings.

"Tasty" Tequila Sunrise Gelato

Prep time: 5 minutes | Cook time: 2 hours 35 minutes | Serves 4-6

- 1/2 cup heavy cream
- 2 cups milk
- 3/4 cup sugar
- I/2 cup orange juice
- 1 teaspoon vanilla extract
- 3 tablespoons tequila
- ½ tablespoon grenadi

1. Refer to note at the beginning of the chapter about freezing bowl.
2. Place the milk and cream in a bowl, and mix them together until well combined. Use a whisk to mix in the sugar. Continue to whisk for about 4 minutes until the sugar dissolves. Then mix in the vanilla extract, orange juice, tequila and grenadine.
3. Pour the ingredients into your ice cream maker, and let it churn for 25 minutes.
4. Put the gelato in an airtight container and place in the freezer for up to 2 hours, until desired consistency is reached.

Pumpkin Gelato

Prep time: 10 minutes | Cook time: 8 minutes | Freeze time: 24 hours | Serves 4

- 3 large egg yolks
- ⅓ cup granulated sugar
- 1 tablespoon light corn syrup
- 1 cup whole milk
- ½ cup heavy cream
- ½ cup canned pumpkin purée
- 1 teaspoon vanilla extract

1. In a small saucepan, add the egg yolks, sugar and corn syrup and beat until well combined.
2. Add the milk, heavy cream, pumpkin purée and pumpkin pie spice and beat until well combined.
3. Place the saucepan over medium heat and cook for about 2-3 minutes, stirring continuously.
4. Remove from the heat and stir in the vanilla extract.
5. Through a fine-mesh strainer, strain the mixture into an empty Ninja CREAMi pint container.
6. Place the container into an ice bath to cool.
7. After cooling, cover the container with the storage lid and freeze for 24 hours.
8. After 24 hours, remove the lid from container and arrange into the outer bowl of Ninja CREAMi.
9. Install the "Creamerizer Paddle" onto the lid of outer bowl.
10. Then rotate the lid clockwise to lock.
11. Press "Power" button to turn on the unit.
12. Then press "GELATO" button.
13. When the program is completed, turn the outer bowl and release it from the machine.
14. Transfer the gelato into bowls and serve immediately.

Banana & Squash Cookie Gelato

Prep time: 5 minutes | Cook time: 3 minutes | Serves 4

- 4 large egg yolks
- 1 cup heavy cream
- ⅓ cup granulated sugar
- ½ of banana, peeled and sliced
- ½ cup frozen butternut squash, chopped
- 1 box instant vanilla pudding mix
- 6 vanilla wafer cookies, crumbled

1. In a small saucepan, add the egg yolks, heavy cream and sugar and beat until well combined.
2. Place the saucepan over medium heat and cook for about 2-3 minutes, stirring continuously.
3. Remove from the heat and through a fine-mesh strainer, strain the mixture into an empty Ninja CREAMi pint container.
4. Place the container into an ice bath to cool.
5. After cooling, add in the banana, squash and pudding until well combined.
6. Cover the container with the storage lid and freeze for 24 hours.
7. After 24 hours, remove the lid from container and arrange into the outer bowl of Ninja CREAMi.
8. Install the "Creamerizer Paddle" onto the lid of outer bowl.
9. Then rotate the lid clockwise to lock.
10. Press "Power" button to turn on the unit.
11. Then press "GELATO" button.
12. When the program is completed, with a spoon, create a 1½-inch wide hole in the center that reaches the bottom of the pint container.
13. Add the wafer cookies into the hole and press "MIX-IN" button.
14. When the program is completed, turn the outer bowl and release it from the machine.
15. Transfer the gelato into serving bowls and serve immediately.

Red Velvet Gelato

Prep time: 5 minutes | Cook time: 3 minutes | Serves 4

- 4 large egg yolks
- ¼ cup granulated sugar
- 2 tablespoons unsweetened cocoa powder
- 1 cup whole milk
- ⅓ cup heavy (whipping) cream
- ¼ cup cream cheese, at room temperature
- 1 teaspoon vanilla extract
- 1 teaspoon red food coloring

1. Fill a large bowl with ice water and set it aside.
2. In a small saucepan, whisk together the egg yolks, sugar, and cocoa powder until everything is fully combined and the sugar is dissolved. Do not do this over heat.
3. Whisk in the milk, heavy cream, cream cheese, vanilla, and food coloring.
4. Place the pan over medium heat. Cook, stirring constantly with a rubber spatula, until the temperature reaches 165°F to 175°F on an instant-read thermometer.
5. Once the base has cooled, place the storage lid on the pint and freeze for 24 hours.
6. Remove the pint from the freezer and take off the lid. Place the pint in the outer bowl of your Ninja CREAMi, install the Creamerizer Paddle in the outer bowl lid, and lock the lid assembly onto the outer bowl. Place the bowl assembly on the motor base, and twist the handle to the right to raise the platform and lock it in place. Select the Gelato function.
7. Once the machine has finished processing, remove the gelato from the pint. Serve immediately.

Peanut Butter Gelato

Prep time: 10 minutes | Cook time: 24 hours | Makes 1 pint

- 1½ cups coconut milk
- 6 tablespoons sugar
- 1 tablespoon cornstarch
- 3 tablespoons peanut butter
- Mix-ins:
- 3 peanut butter cups, chopped

1. Add all the ingredients except peanut butter and mix-ins to a saucepan over medium heat.
2. Bring to a boil.
3. Reduce heat to low and simmer for 3 minutes, stirring constantly.
4. Stir in the peanut butter.
5. Pour mixture into your Ninja Creami pint container.
6. Freeze for 24 hours.
7. Add the container to the machine.
8. Press the Gelato function.
9. Add the peanut butter cups.
10. Press the Mix-in mode.

Sweet Potato Gelato

Prep time: 10 minutes | Cook time: 8 minutes | Freeze time: 24 hours | Serves 4

- ½ cup canned sweet potato purée
- 4 large egg yolks
- ¼ cup sugar
- ½ teaspoon ground cinnamon
- ⅛ teaspoon ground nutmeg
- 1 cup heavy cream
- 1 teaspoon vanilla extract

1. In a small saucepan, add the sweet potato purée, egg yolks, sugar, ½ teaspoon of cinnamon and nutmeg and beat until well combined.
2. Add the heavy cream and vanilla extract and beat until well combined.
3. Place the saucepan over medium heat and cook for about 2-3 minutes, stirring continuously.
4. Remove from the heat and through a fine-mesh strainer, strain the mixture into an empty Ninja CREAMi pint container.
5. Place the container into an ice bath to cool.
6. After cooling, cover the container with the storage lid and freeze for 24 hours.
7. After 24 hours, remove the lid from container and arrange into the outer bowl of Ninja CREAMi.
8. Install the "Creamerizer Paddle" onto the lid of outer bowl.
9. Then rotate the lid clockwise to lock.
10. Press "Power" button to turn on the unit.
11. Then press "GELATO" button.
12. When the program is completed, turn the outer bowl and release it from the machine.
13. Transfer the gelato into bowls and serve immediately.

Black Cherry Gelato

Prep time: 40 minutes | Cook time: 24 hours | Makes 1 pint

- 4 egg yolks
- 5 tablespoons granulated sugar
- 1 tablespoon corn syrup
- 1 cup heavy cream
- ⅓ cup milk
- 1 teaspoon almond extract
- 1 cup black cherries, sliced

1. Add the egg yolks, sugar and corn syrup to a saucepan.
2. Mix well.
3. Stir in the heavy cream, almond extract and milk.
4. Place the pan over medium heat.
5. Cook until temperature has reached 165 degrees F.
6. Strain the mixture into the Ninja Creami pint container.
7. Freeze for 24 hours.
8. Place in the machine.
9. Press the Gelato function.

Cherry Gelato

Prep time: 10 minutes | Cook time: 8 minutes | Freeze time: 24 hours |Serves 4

- 4 large egg yolks
- 1 tablespoon light corn syrup
- 5 tablespoons granulated sugar
- 1 cup heavy cream
- ⅓ cup whole milk
- 1 teaspoon almond extract
- 1 cup frozen black cherries, pitted and quartered

1. In a small saucepan, add the egg yolks, sugar and corn syrup and beat until well combined.
2. Add the heavy cream, milk and almond extract and beat until well combined.
3. Place the saucepan over medium heat and cook for about 2-3 minutes, stirring continuously.
4. Remove from the heat and through a fine-mesh strainer, strain the mixture into an empty Ninja CREAMi pint container.
5. Place the container into an ice bath to cool.
6. After cooling, cover the container with the storage lid and freeze for 24 hours.
7. After 24 hours, remove the lid from container and arrange into the outer bowl of Ninja CREAMi.
8. Install the "Creamerizer Paddle" onto the lid of outer bowl.
9. Then rotate the lid clockwise to lock.
10. Press "Power" button to turn on the unit.
11. Then press "GELATO" button.
12. When the program is completed, with a spoon, create a 1½-inch wide hole in the center that reaches the bottom of the pint container.
13. Add the cherries into the hole and press "MIX-IN" button.
14. When the program is completed, turn the outer bowl and release it from the machine.
15. Transfer the gelato into bowls and serve immediately.

Butter Pecan Gelato

Prep time: 15 minutes | Cook time: 24 hours | Makes 1 pint

- 4 egg yolks
- 5 tablespoons granulated sugar
- 1 tablespoon corn syrup
- 1 teaspoon butter flavor extract
- ⅓ cup milk
- ⅓ cup pecans, chopped

1. Add the egg yolks, sugar and corn syrup to a pan over medium heat.
2. Stir in the cream, butter extract and milk.
3. Cook while stirring until the temperature has reached 165 degrees F.
4. Transfer mixture to your Ninja Creami pint container.
5. Freeze for 24 hours.
6. Add the container to the machine.
7. Choose the Gelato function.
8. Stir in the pecans.
9. Press the Mix-in function.

Spirulina Cookie Gelato

Prep time: 5 minutes | Cook time: 3 minutes | Serves 4

- 4 large egg yolks
- ⅓ cup granulated sugar
- 1 up oat milk
- 1 teaspoon vanilla extract
- 1 teaspoon blue spirulina powder
- 4 small crunchy chocolate chip cookies, crumbled

1. In a small saucepan, add the egg yolks and sugar and beat until well combined.
2. Add oat milk and vanilla extract and stir to combine.
3. Place the saucepan over medium heat and cook for about 2-3 minutes, stirring continuously.
4. Remove from the heat and through a fine-mesh strainer, strain the mixture into an empty Ninja CREAMi pint container.
5. Place the container into an ice bath to cool.
6. After cooling, cover the container with the storage lid and freeze for 24 hours.
7. After 24 hours, remove the lid from container and arrange into the outer bowl of Ninja CREAMi.
8. Install the "Creamerizer Paddle" onto the lid of outer bowl.
9. Then rotate the lid clockwise to lock.
10. Press "Power" button to turn on the unit.
11. Then press "GELATO" button.
12. When the program is completed, with a spoon, create a 1½-inch wide hole in the center that reaches the bottom of the pint container.
13. Add the chocolate chip cookies into the hole and press "MIX-IN" button.
14. When the program is completed, turn the outer bowl and release it from the machine.
15. Transfer the gelato into serving bowls and serve immediately.

Chapter 6
Smoothie Bowls Recipes

Frozen Fruit Smoothie Bowl

Prep time: 5 minutes | Cook time: 3 minutes | Serves 2

- 1 ripe banana, peeled and cut in 1-inch pieces
- 2 cups frozen fruit mix
- 1¼ cups vanilla yogurt

1. In a large high-speed blender, add all the ingredients and pulse until smooth.
2. Transfer the mixture into an empty Ninja CREAMi pint container.
3. Cover the container with the storage lid and freeze for 24 hours.
4. After 24 hours, remove the lid from container and arrange into the outer bowl of Ninja CREAMi.
5. Install the "Creamerizer Paddle" onto the lid of outer bowl.
6. Then rotate the lid clockwise to lock.
7. Press "Power" button to turn on the unit.
8. Then press "SMOOTHIE BOWL" button.
9. When the program is completed, turn the outer bowl and release it from the machine.
10. Transfer the smoothie into serving bowls and serve immediately.

Peach & Grapefruit Smoothie Bowl

Prep time: 5 minutes | Cook time: 3 minutes | Serves 2

- 1 cup frozen peach pieces
- 1 cup vanilla Greek yogurt
- ¼ cup fresh grapefruit juice
- 2 tablespoons honey
- ¼ teaspoon vanilla extract
- ½ teaspoon ground cinnamon

1. In a high-speed blender, add all ingredients and pulse until smooth
2. Transfer the mixture into an empty Ninja CREAMi pint container.
3. Cover the container with the storage lid and freeze for 24 hours.
4. After 24 hours, remove the lid from container and arrange into the outer bowl of Ninja CREAMi.
5. Install the "Creamerizer Paddle" onto the lid of outer bowl.
6. Then rotate the lid clockwise to lock.
7. Press "Power" button to turn on the unit.
8. Then press "SMOOTHIE BOWL" button.
9. When the program is completed, turn the outer bowl and release it from the machine.
10. Transfer the smoothie into serving bowls and serve immediately.

Papaya Smoothie Bowl

Prep time: 5 minutes | Cook time: 3 minutes | Serves 2

- 2 cups ripe papaya, peeled and cut into 1-inch pieces
- 14 ounces (397 g) whole milk
- 4-6 drops liquid stevia
- ¼ teaspoon vanilla extract

1. Place the mango pieces into an empty Ninja CREAMi pint container.
2. Top with coconut milk, stevia and vanilla extract and stir to combine.
3. Cover the container with the storage lid and freeze for 24 hours.
4. After 24 hours, remove the lid from container and arrange into the outer bowl of Ninja CREAMi.
5. Install the "Creamerizer Paddle" onto the lid of outer bowl.
6. Then rotate the lid clockwise to lock.
7. Press "Power" button to turn on the unit.
8. Then press "SMOOTHIE BOWL" button.
9. When the program is completed, turn the outer bowl and release it from the machine.
10. Transfer the smoothie into serving bowls and serve immediately.

Pitaya Pineapple Smoothie Bowl

Prep time: 10 minutes | Cook time: 10 minutes | Freeze time: 24 hours | Serves 4

- 2 cups frozen pitaya chunks
- 1 can pineapple juice

1. Mix the pitaya chunks and pineapple juice until well combined in a large bowl.
2. Transfer the mixture into an empty Ninja CREAMi Pint.
3. Cover the pint with the lid and freeze for 24 hours.
4. After 24 hours, remove the lid from the pint and place it into the outer bowl of the Ninja CREAMi.
5. Install the Creamerizer Paddle onto the lid of the outer bowl, then rotate the lid clockwise to lock.
6. Turn the unit on.
7. Press the SMOOTHIE BOWL button.
8. When the program is complete, turn the outer bowl and release it from the machine.
9. Transfer the smoothie into serving bowls and serve with your favorite toppings.

Kale, Avocado & fruit Smoothie Bowl

Prep time: 10 minutes | Cook time: 15 minutes | Freeze time: 24 hours | Serves 4

- 1 banana, peeled and cut into 1-inch pieces
- ½ of avocado, peeled, pitted and cut into 1-inch pieces
- 1 cup fresh kale leaves
- 1 cup green apple, peeled, cored and cut into 1-inch pieces
- ¼ cup unsweetened coconut milk
- 2 tablespoons agave nectar

1. In a large high-speed blender, add all the ingredients and pulse until smooth.
2. Transfer the mixture into an empty Ninja CREAMi pint container.
3. Cover the container with storage lid and freeze for 24 hours.
4. After 24 hours, remove the lid from container and arrange into the Outer Bowl of Ninja CREAMi.
5. Install the Creamerizer Paddle onto the lid of Outer Bowl.
6. Then rotate the lid clockwise to lock.
7. Press Power button to turn on the unit.
8. Then press Smoothie Bowl button.
9. When the program is completed, turn the Outer Bowl and release it from the machine.
10. Transfer the smoothie into serving bowls and serve immediately.

Pear Smoothie Bowl

Prep time: 10 minutes | Cook time: 10 minutes | Freeze time: 24 hours | Serves 3

- 2 cups fresh pear
- ½ cup apple cider
- 2 tablespoons protein powder
- ¼ cup pecans
- 1 cup ice
- ½ cup Greek yogurt
- 2 cups milk

1. Blitz the pear with the remaining ingredients in a blender until smooth.
2. Move this mixture to the MAX FILL line of a CREAMi pint.
3. Fasten the lid of the pint and freeze for 24 hours.
4. After 24 hours, open the pint, fix it into the outer bowl of Ninja CREAMi along with the 'Creamerizer paddle'
5. Fasten the lid, turn on the 'Power Button', and select the 'SMOOTHIE BOWL' function.
6. Dish out the smoothie from the pint and serve as desired.

Berry & Yogurt Smoothie

Prep time: 5 minutes | Cook time: 24 hours | Serves 1

- 1 cup raspberries, sliced
- 1 cup blackberries, sliced
- 1 cup strawberries, sliced
- 2 tablespoons raw agave nectar
- ¼ cup vanilla yogurt

1. Place all the ingredients in a bowl.
2. Mix well.
3. Pour the mixture into the Ninja Creami pint container.
4. Freeze for 24 hours.
5. Place the container in the machine.
6. Hit Smoothie function.

Tropical Banana Smoothie

Prep time: 5 minutes | Cook time: 24 hours | Serves 1

- 2 bananas, sliced
- 1 cup pineapple, diced
- ¼ cup yogurt
- 2 tablespoons honey

1. Add all the ingredients to Ninja Creami pint container.
2. Freeze for 24 hours.
3. Transfer the container in the machine.
4. Press Smoothie function.

Avocado Kale Smoothie

Prep time: 5 minutes | Cook time: 24 hours | Serves 1

- ½ avocado, pitted and sliced
- 1 banana, sliced
- 1 cup green apple, sliced
- 1 cup kale leaves
- ¼ cup coconut milk
- 2 tablespoons honey

1. Add the avocado, banana, green apple and kale to a blender.
2. Blend until smooth.
3. Transfer the mixture to the Ninja Creami pint container.
4. Freeze for 24 hours.
5. Place it in the machine.
6. Process using the Smoothie function.

Coconut Mango Smoothie

Prep time: 5 minutes | Cook time: 24 hours | Serves 4

- 2 cups ripe mango, peeled and sliced
- 14 oz. coconut milk

1. Add the mango and coconut milk to the Ninja Creami pint container.
2. Freeze for 24 hours.
3. Transfer the container in the machine.
4. Press Smoothie function.

Peach Mango Smoothie

Prep time: 5 minutes | Cook time: 3 minutes | Serves 4

- 5 peaches, peeled and pitted
- 3 cups frozen mango
- ½ teaspoon ground turmeric
- 1 scoop vanilla protein powder
- 1 cup orange or mango juice
- Water, as needed

1. In a high-speed blender or food processor, combine all the ingredients, adding water to loosen the frozen mixture if necessary.
2. Enjoy!

Raspberry Coconut Smoothie

Prep time: 5 minutes | Cook time: 3 minutes | Serves 4

- 4 cups frozen raspberries
- Juice of ½ a lemon
- 1 cup coconut milk
- 2 tablespoons honey
- Water, as needed

1. In a high-speed blender, combine all the ingredients and mix until smooth.
2. Serve immediately in chilled glasses.

Very Berry Smoothie

Prep time: 5 minutes | Cook time: 3 minutes | Serves 4

- 5 cups frozen mixed berries
- 1 large banana
- 1 cup almond milk (optional)
- 1 tablespoon chia seeds
- 1 tablespoon maple syrup
- Water, as needed

1. In a high-speed blender or food processor, combine all the ingredients, adding water to loosen the frozen mixture if necessary.
2. Enjoy!

Matcha Green Tea Smoothie

Prep time: 5 minutes | Cook time: 3 minutes | Serves 2

- 2 bananas, frozen
- 2 teaspoons matcha powder
- 1 avocado, pitted and cubed
- 1 cup kale, chopped
- 1 cup almond milk (optional)

1. In a high-speed blender or food processor, combine all the ingredients, adding water to loosen the frozen mixture if necessary.
2. Enjoy!

Green Fruity Smoothie Bowl

Prep time: 5 minutes | Cook time: 5 minutes | Serves 2

- 1 banana, peeled and cut into 1-inch pieces
- ½ of avocado, peeled, pitted and cut into 1-inch pieces
- 1 cup fresh kale leaves
- 1 cup green apple, peeled, cored and cut into 1-inch pieces
- ¼ cup unsweetened coconut milk
- 2 tablespoons agave nectar

1. In a large high-speed blender, add all the ingredients and pulse until smooth.
2. Transfer the mixture into an empty Ninja CREAMi pint container.
3. Cover the container with the storage lid and freeze for 24 hours.
4. After 24 hours, remove the lid from container and arrange into the outer bowl of Ninja CREAMi.
5. Install the "Creamerizer Paddle" onto the lid of outer bowl.
6. Then rotate the lid clockwise to lock.
7. Press "Power" button to turn on the unit.
8. Then press "SMOOTHIE BOWL" button.
9. When the program is completed, turn the outer bowl and release it from the machine.
10. Transfer the smoothie into serving bowls and serve immediately.

Honey Berry Smoothie Bowl

Prep time: 10 minutes | Cook time: 10 minutes | Freeze time: 24 hours | Serves 4

- 1 cup fresh blueberries
- 1 cup fresh blackberries
- 1 cup fresh raspberries
- ¼ cup yogurt
- 1 tablespoon honey

1. Mix all the ingredients until well combined in a large bowl.
2. Transfer the mixture into an empty Ninja CREAMi Pint.
3. Cover the pint with the lid and freeze for 24 hours.
4. After 24 hours, remove the lid and place the pint into the outer bowl of the Ninja CREAMi.
5. Install the Creamerizer Paddle onto the lid of the outer bowl, then rotate the lid clockwise to lock.
6. Turn the unit on.
7. Press the SMOOTHIE BOWL button.
8. When the program is complete, turn the outer bowl and release it from the machine.
9. Transfer the smoothie into serving bowls and serve with your favorite toppings.

Cranberries Yogurt Smoothie Bowl

Prep time: 5 minutes | Cook time: 10 minutes | Freeze time: 24 hours | Serves 1

- ¼ cup vanilla yogurt
- 1 cup fresh cranberries
- 3 tablespoons orange juice
- 1 tablespoon sugar

1. Move all the ingredients to the MAX FILL line of a CREAMi pint.
2. Fasten the lid of the pint and freeze for 24 hours.
3. After 24 hours, open the pint, fix it into the outer bowl of Ninja CREAMi along with the 'Creamerizer paddle'
4. Fasten the lid, turn on the 'Power Button', and select the 'SMOOTHIE BOWL" function.
5. Dish out the smoothie from the pint and serve as desired.

Simple Smoothie Bowl

Prep time: 5 minutes | Cook time: 5 minutes | Serves 2

- 1 bottle fruit smoothie beverage

1. Pour the smoothie beverage into a clean CREAMi Pint. Place the storage lid on the container and freeze for 24 hours
2. Remove the pint from the freezer and take off the lid. Place the pint in the outer bowl of your Ninja CREAMi, install the Creamerizer Paddle in the outer bowl lid, and lock the lid assembly onto the outer bowl. Place the bowl assembly on the motor base, and twist the handle to the right to raise the platform and lock it in place. Select the Smoothie Bowl function.
3. Once the machine has finished processing, remove the smoothie bowl from the pint. Serve immediately with desired toppings.

Pumpkin Smoothie Bowl

Prep time: 10 minutes | Cook time: 10 minutes | Freeze time: 24 hours | Serves 2

- 1 cup canned pumpkin puree
- ⅓ cup plain Greek yogurt
- 1½ tablespoons maple syrup
- 1 teaspoon vanilla extract
- 1 teaspoon pumpkin pie spice
- 1 frozen banana, peeled and cut in ½-inch pieces

1. In an empty Ninja CREAMi pint container, add the pumpkin puree, yogurt, maple syrup, vanilla extract and pumpkin pie spice and mix well.
2. Add the banana pieces and stir to combine.
3. Transfer the mixture into an empty Ninja CREAMi pint container.
4. Arrange the container into the Outer Bowl of Ninja CREAMi.
5. Install the Creamerizer Paddle onto the lid of Outer Bowl.
6. Then rotate the lid clockwise to lock.
7. Press Power button to turn on the unit.
8. Then press Smoothie Bowl button.
9. When the program is completed, turn the Outer Bowl and release it from the machine.
10. Transfer the smoothie into serving bowls and serve immediately.

Strawberry Smoothie Bowl

Prep time: 10 minutes | Cook time: 10 minutes | Freeze time: 24 hours | Serves 4

- ¼ cup agave nectar
- 2 tablespoons vanilla protein powder
- 1 cup ripe banana, peeled and cut in ½-inch pieces
- ½ cup whole milk
- ¼ cup pineapple juice
- 1 cup fresh strawberries, hulled and quartered

1. Combine the milk with agave nectar, vanilla protein powder and pineapple juice in a bowl. Place the banana and strawberry in a CREAMi pint and press them firmly below the MAX FILL line.
2. Top with milk mixture and stir well.
3. Fasten the lid of the pint and freeze for 24 hours.
4. After 24 hours, open the pint, fix it into the outer bowl of Ninja CREAMi along with the 'Creamerizer paddle'
5. Fasten the lid, turn on the 'Power Button', and select the 'SMOOTHIE BOWL" function.
6. Dish out the smoothie from the pint and serve as desired.

Raspberry Melon Baobab Smoothie

Prep time: 5 minutes | Cook time:5 minutes |Serves 2

- Smoothie
- ½ cup frozen raspberries
- 1 cup frozen cantaloupe chunks
- 1 cup unsweetened almond milk
- 1 scoop vanilla protein powder
- 1 teaspoon baobab powder
- ½ teaspoon psyllium husks
- 2 tablespoons peanut butter (crunchy or smooth, optional)
- A few ice cubes
- Toppings
- 2 tablespoons blueberries
- 2 tablespoons toasted shredded coconut
- 1 tablespoon cacao nibs

1. Blend all the smoothie ingredients together, until a desired consistency is achieved.
2. Top with vibrant blueberries, coconut and cacao nibs and slurp. I mean eat!

Coffee Smoothie Bowl

Prep time: 5 minutes | Cook time: 5 minutes | Freeze time: 24 hours | Serves 1

SMOOTHIE BOWL:

- 1 cup coffee (brewed; not just the coffee beans or grounds)
- ½ cup oat milk
- 2 tablespoons mocha almond butter
- 1 cup raspberries
- 1 banana
- Toppings:
- 1 banana
- ½ cup raspberries
- 1 tablespoon sliced almonds
- ¼ cup chocolate-covered espresso beans
- 1 teaspoon honey
- Maple syrup

1. Combine all ingredients in a blender and blend until smooth.
2. Pour into an empty ninja CREAMi Pint container and freeze for 24 hours.
3. After 24 hours, remove the Pint from the freezer. Remove the lid.
4. Place the Ninja CREAMi Pint into the outer bowl. Place the outer bowl with the Pint in it into the ninja CREAMi machine and turn until the outer bowl locks into place. Push the SMOOTHIE button. During the SMOOTHIE function, the ingredients will mix together and become very creamy.
5. Once the SMOOTHIE function has ended, turn the outer bowl and release it from the ninja CREAMi machine.
6. Scoop the smoothie into a bowl. Drizzle with maple syrup or honey. Top with sliced almonds, chocolate-covered coffee beans, raspberries, and sliced bananas.
7. Your smoothie bowl is ready to eat!

Mango Lucama Super-Green Smoothie

Prep time: 5 minutes | Cook time:5 minutes |Serves 2

- Smoothie
- 1 cup soy milk
- ½ cup frozen mango
- 1 scoop vanilla protein powder (about 30g)
- 2 teaspoons lucama powder
- ½ teaspoon Spirulina powder
- ½ avocado
- ¼ cup kale leaves
- ¼ cup spinach
- Few ice cubes
- Toppings
- ½ kiwi, sliced
- 5 strawberries, sliced
- 1 tablespoon goji berries
- 1 tablespoon chia seeds
- 1 tablespoon cacao nibs

1. Place all the smoothie ingredients in to the blender and rev it up until all the ingredients are thoroughly incorporated! You can add cold water if you want a thinner consistency.
2. Play with the toppings and turn your bowl into a piece of art!

Pineapple, Banana, and Peach Smoothie Bowl

Prep time: 5 minutes | Cook time:5 minutes |Serves 1

- Smoothie
- ½ cup vanilla almond milk
- ¼ cup oats
- 1 cup pineapple, cut into chunks
- 1 peach, pitted
- 1 banana, frozen
- 1 small piece candied ginger
- ½ cup Greek yogurt
- Toppings
- 2 tablespoons sunflower seeds
- ¼ cup blueberries
- 1 tablespoon honey
- Peach slices

1. Toss all the smoothie ingredients into the blender and mix on high speed, until a smooth puree is formed.
2. Transfer to a bowl and top generously with the scrumptious topping assortments.

Dark Cherry Smoothie Bowl

Prep time: 5 minutes | Cook time:5 minutes |Serves 1

- Smoothie
- 2 cups frozen cherries, pitted
- 1 banana
- ¾ cup coconut water
- 2 scoops vanilla protein powder
- Topping
- 8 whole cherries
- ¼ cup coconut flakes
- ¼ cup sliced almonds
- ¼ cup raw cacao nibs

1. Blend all the smoothie ingredients, until a smooth lump-free consistency is formed.
2. Pour into a bowl and sprinkle with the gorgeously contrasting toppings to set off the exquisite red of the smoothie!
3. Grab a spoon and dig in (or slurp!).

Berry Smoothie Bowl with Peach and Orange

Prep time: 5 minutes | Cook time:5 minutes |Serves 1

- Smoothie
- 1 ½ cups frozen peaches
- 1 banana
- ½ cup orange juice, chilled (fresh squeezed, preferably)
- ½ cup blackberries
- ½ cup frozen blueberries
- Toppings
- ¼ cup walnuts
- 2 tablespoon hemp seeds
- Honey
- 2 tablespoons dried mulberries

1. Blend all the smoothie ingredients until a rich ice cream consistency is achieved.
2. Transfer to a bowl and sprinkle with chopped walnuts, mulberries, hemp seeds and a drizzle of honey!

Blueberry Cacao Smoothie Bowl

Prep time: 5 minutes | Cook time:5 minutes |Serves 2

- Smoothie
- 1¼ cups unsweetened vanilla almond milk
- 1 cup frozen blueberries
- 1 cup frozen spinach
- 1 tablespoon cacao powder
- 1 tablespoon hemp seeds
- 2 Medjool dates
- 1 scoop vanilla brown rice protein
- A few drops of vanilla extract
- Toppings
- 1 tablespoon coconut flakes
- 2 tablespoons cacao nibs
- 2 tablespoons goji berries
- 2 tablespoons blueberries
- 1 granola bar, crumbled

1. Blend all smoothie ingredients, until a smooth creamy puree is formed.
2. Transfer to a bowl and play with the toppings!

Very Berry Cherry Smoothie Bowl

Prep time: 10 minutes | Cook time: 10 minutes | Freeze time: 24 hours | Serves 4

- 2 cups frozen cherry berry blend
- 1 cup cranberry juice cocktail
- ¼ cup raw agave nectar

1. Mix all the ingredients until well combined in a large bowl.
2. Transfer the mixture into an empty Ninja CREAMi Pint.
3. Cover the pint with the lid and freeze for 24 hours.
4. After 24 hours, remove the lid and place the pint into the outer bowl of the Ninja CREAMi.
5. Install the Creamerizer Paddle onto the lid of the outer bowl, then rotate the lid clockwise to lock.
6. Turn the unit on.
7. Press the SMOOTHIE BOWL button.
8. When the program is complete, turn the outer bowl and release it from the machine.
9. Transfer the smoothie into serving bowls and serve with your favorite toppings.

Lime Beer Sorbet

Prep time: 5 minutes | Cook time: 5 minutes | Serves 4

- ¾ cup beer
- ⅔ cup water
- ½ cup fresh lime juice
- ¼ cup granulated sugar

1. In a high-speed blender, add all the ingredients and pulse until smooth.
2. Set aside for about 5 minutes.
3. Transfer the mixture into an empty Ninja CREAMi pint container.
4. Cover the container with the storage lid and freeze for 24 hours.
5. After 24 hours, remove the lid from container and arrange into the outer bowl of Ninja CREAMi.
6. Install the "Creamerizer Paddle" onto the lid of outer bowl.
7. Then rotate the lid clockwise to lock.
8. Press "Power" button to turn on the unit.
9. Then press "SORBET" button.
10. When the program is completed, turn the outer bowl and release it from the machine
11. Transfer the sorbet into serving bowls and serve immediately.

Pina Colada Sorbet

Prep time: 5 minutes | Cook time: 24 hours | Makes 1 pint

- 15 oz. canned crushed pineapples
- 3 tablespoons coconut cream
- ¼ cup creamer

1. Pour all the ingredients into the Ninja Creami pint container.
2. Stir to combine.
3. Freeze for 24 hours.
4. Place in the machine.
5. Choose the Sorbet function.

Cuddling Cucumber Basil Rum Sorbet

Prep time: 5 minutes | Cook time: 2 hours 35 minutes | Serves 8

- 4 cups chopped cucumbers
- ½ cup basil
- ½ cup honey
- 4 tablespoons rum

1. Refer to note at the beginning of the chapter about freezing bowl.
2. Use a food processor or blender to puree all the ingredients until smooth.
3. Pour the ingredients into your ice cream maker, and let it churn for 25-30 minutes.
4. Place in an airtight container for up to 2 hours, until desired consistency is reached.

Caribbean Pineapple Mint Sorbet

Prep time: 5 minutes | Cook time: 2 hours 40 minutes | Serves 9

- 1 diced, peeled, and cored small pineapple
- 2 tablespoons lemon juice
- ½ cup mint
- 1 cup plus 2 tablespoons sugar

1. Puree the pineapple, mint and lemon juice in a food processor or blender. Then add in the sugar and puree until the sugar dissolves.
2. Pour the ingredients into your ice cream maker, and let it churn for 25-30 minutes.
3. Place in an airtight container for up to 2 hours, until desired consistency is reached.

Apple Sorbet

Prep time: 5 minutes | Cook time: 5 minutes | Serves 3

- 5 frozen apples, peeled, cored and deseeded
- 3 tablespoons fresh pressed apple juice
- 1/2 teaspoon lemon juice

1. Place a large mixing bowl under the Yonanas chute and push the apples through.
2. Add apple and lemon juice.
3. Stir until smooth.
4. Spoon into individual bowls and freeze leftovers in an airtight container.

Luscious Lavender Sour Cherry Sorbet

Prep time: 5 minutes | Cook time: 5 hours 35 minutes | Serves 6

- 3 cups pitted, sliced sour cherries
- ½ teaspoon lavender
- 3/4 cup sugar
- 1/2 teaspoon salt
- 2 tablespoons vanilla extract
- 2 ½ teaspoons lime juice

1. Refer to note at the beginning of the chapter about freezing bowl.
2. Use a food processor or blender to puree the lavender, sugar, cherries, and vanilla extract. Then blend in the salt and lime juice. Strain the mixture into a bowl, and refrigerate covered for 2-3 hours.
3. Pour the ingredients into your ice cream maker, and let it churn for 25-30 minutes.
4. Place in an airtight container for up to 2 hours, until desired consistency is reached.

Lemon Mint Melon Sorbet

Prep time: 5 minutes | Cook time: 3 hours 10 minutes | Serves 4

- ½ cup lemon juice
- 1 cup boiling water
- 1 cup chopped mint
- ½ cup melon
- Zest of 1 lemon
- 1 cup sugar

1. Mix together the sugar, lemon zest, mint and melon in a heat safe bowl. Then pour in the water, and stir frequently until sugar dissolves. Let the mixture sit for 20 minutes. Then strain it into another bowl. Mix in the lemon juice and let the mixture cool totally.
2. Pour the ingredients into your ice cream maker, and let it churn for 25-30 minutes.
3. Place in an airtight container for up to 2 hours, until desired consistency is reached.

Strawberry, Nectarine, Orange, Banana Sorbet

Prep time: 5 minutes | Cook time: 10 minutes | Serves 8

- ¾ cup sugar
- ¾ cup water
- 1 cup strawberries, hulled
- 1 cup orange wedges, peeled and seeds removed
- 1 cup nectarine, peeled and seeds removed
- 1 ripe banana, peeled

1. Place the water and sugar in a saucepan. Bring to a boil until the sugar dissolves.
2. Remove from the heat and place in the fridge to chill for at least 3 hours.
3. Place the rest of the ingredients in a blender and add the chilled sugar mixture. Pulse until smooth. Allow to chill for another two hours.
4. Turn on the Cuisinart and pour in the mixture.
5. Churn for 10 minutes.
6. Transfer in an airtight container and freeze overnight.

Summer Sorbet

Prep time: 5 minutes | Cook time: 15 minutes | Serves 6

- 2 pounds fresh fruit of your choice
- 8 ounces sugar
- ¼ cup lemon juice
- ¼ cup vodka

1. Place all ingredients in a blender. Pulse until smooth.
2. Place in the fridge and allow to chill for at least 3 hours.
3. Turn on the Cuisinart and pour in the mixture.
4. Churn for 10 minutes.
5. Transfer in an airtight container and freeze overnight.

Rosé Sherbet

Prep time: 5 minutes | Cook time: 5 minutes | Serves 3-5

- 3 cups frozen raspberries
- 1/2 cup rosé wine
- Rose petals forgarnish

1. Place a large mixing bowl under the Yonanas chute and push the raspberries through.
2. Add rosé wine and mix until well-blended
3. Scoop into champagneglasses and add a rose petal or two forgarnish.

Pineapple Basil Sorbet

Prep time: 10 minutes | Cook time: 10 minutes | Freeze time: 24 hours | Serves 6

- 16 ounces canned pineapple chunks, with juice
- 1 teaspoon lemon juice
- 1 teaspoon lemon zest
- 1 small piece of ginger, sliced
- 1 teaspoon basil leaves
- ⅓ cup white caster sugar

1. Place all the ingredients in a blender. Mix well until smooth.
2. Pour the mixture into the Ninja CREAMi Pint and close the lid.
3. Place the pint into the freezer and freeze for 24 hours.
4. Once done, open the lid, place the pint into the outer bowl of the Ninja CREAMi, and set the Creamerizer Paddle into the outer bowl.
5. Lock the lid by rotating it clockwise.
6. Turn the unit on and press the SORBET button.
7. Once done, take out the bowl from the Ninja CREAMi.
8. Serve and enjoy this yummy sorbet.

Vanilla Rhubarb Sorbet

Prep time: 10 minutes | Cook time: 10 minutes | Freeze time: 24 hours | Serves 6

- 3 cups rhubarb, chopped
- ½ teaspoon vanilla extract
- 2/3 cup golden caster sugar
- 3 tablespoons liquid glucose
- 2 teaspoons star anise
- 1 cup lemon juice

1. Add the ingredients to a blender. Mix well until smooth.
2. Pour the mixture into the Ninja CREAMi Pint and close the lid.
3. Place the pint into the freezer and freeze for 24 hours.
4. Once done, open the lid and place the pint into the outer bowl of the Ninja CREAMi. Set the Creamerizer Paddle into the outer bowl.
5. Lock the lid by rotating it clockwise.
6. Turn the unit on and press the SORBET button.
7. Once done, take out the bowl from the Ninja CREAMi.
8. Serve and enjoy this yummy sorbet.

Spiced Apple Cider Sorbet

Prep time: 5 minutes | Cook time: 5 minutes | Serves 2-4

- 6 frozen apples, peeled, cored and seeded
- 3 tablespoons fresh pressed apple juice
- 1 teaspoon honey
- 1 teaspoongrated cloves
- 2 teaspoons cinnamon
- 1/2 teaspoon fresh lemon juice
- 2 tablespoons spiced rum

1. Place a large mixing bowl under the Yonanas chute and push the apples through.
2. Add apple juice, honey, clove, cinnamon, lemon juice and spiced rum to the mixing bowl.
3. Mix until smooth to blend the flavors.
4. Spoon into individual bowls.
5. Freeze leftovers in an airtight container.

Lemon Drop Sorbet

Prep time: 5 minutes | Cook time: 5 minutes | Serves 2

- 4 frozen bananas, peeled
- 4 tablespoons fresh lemon juice, frozen
- 3 tablespoons lemon zest
- 1 teaspoon honey
- 1 tablespoon vodka
- 1/2 teaspoon pink Himalayan salt

1. Place a large mixing bowl under the Yonanas chute.
2. Push the frozen bananas through the chute.
3. Add frozen lemon juice, zest, honey, vodka and salt to mixing bowl.
4. Mix until well-blended.
5. Spoon into individual bowls.
6. Freeze leftovers in an airtight container.

Acai & Fruit Sorbet

Prep time: 5 minutes | Cook time: 5 minutes | Serves 4

- 1 packet frozen acai
- ½ cup blackberries
- ½ cup banana, peeled and sliced
- ¼ cup granulated sugar
- 1 cup water

1. In a high-speed blender, add all the ingredients and pulse until smooth.
2. Transfer the mixture into an empty Ninja CREAMi pint container.
3. Cover the container with storage lid and freeze for 24 hours.
4. After 24 hours, remove the lid from container and arrange into the Outer Bowl of Ninja CREAMi.
5. Install the Creamerizer Paddle onto the lid of Outer Bowl.
6. Then rotate the lid clockwise to lock.
7. Press Power button to turn on the unit.
8. Then press Sorbet button.
9. When the program is completed, turn the Outer Bowl and release it from the machine.
10. Transfer the sorbet into serving bowls and serve immediately.

Strawberry & Beet Sorbet

Prep time: 5 minutes | Cook time: 5 minutes | Serves 4

- 2⅔ cups strawberries, hulled and quartered
- ⅓ cup cooked beets, quartered
- ⅓ cup granulated sugar
- ⅓ cup orange juice

1. In a high-speed blender, add mangoes and beets and pulse until smooth.
2. Through a fine-mesh strainer, strain the mango puree into a large bowl.
3. Add the sugar and orange juice and and stir to combine.
4. Transfer the mixture into an empty Ninja CREAMi pint container.
5. Cover the container with the storage lid and freeze for 24 hours.
6. After 24 hours, remove the lid from container and arrange into the outer bowl of Ninja CREAMi.
7. Install the "Creamerizer Paddle" onto the lid of outer bowl.
8. Then rotate the lid clockwise to lock.
9. Press "Power" button to turn on the unit.
10. Then press "SORBET" button.
11. When the program is completed, turn the outer bowl and release it from the machine.
12. Transfer the sorbet into serving bowls and serve immediately.

Blueberry Ginger Sorbet

Prep time: 5 minutes | Cook time: 3 minutes |Serves 4

- 5 cups fresh blueberries
- 2 teaspoons lemon juice
- 1 tablespoon fresh ginger, minced
- 1 cup sugar
- 1 pinch kosher salt
- ¼ cup water

1. In a blender or food processor, place the blueberries, the lemon juice | Sugar:, and water.
2. Purée until smooth, about 3 minutes.
3. Pour the mixture in a Pyrex or stainless steel 9x13 pan and freeze for 30 minutes. The edges should start freezing.
4. Using a handheld electric mixer, beat the sorbet for 1 minute, or until smooth.
5. Return the sorbet to the freezer for another 30 minutes and beat again as before. Repeat this step 4–5 times, until the sorbet is firm.
6. Serve right away or transfer the sorbet to an airtight freezer-safe container.

Black Forest Sorbet

Prep time: 5 minutes | Cook time:5 minutes |Serves 4

- ¼ cup granulated sugar
- ¼ cup water
- 2 tablespoons cocoa powder
- 1 cup almond milk
- 3 cups pitted sweet cherries

1. In a saucepan over medium heat, combine the water and sugar and bring to a boil.
2. Cook for about 5 minutes, and then let it cool.
3. Combine all the smoothie ingredients in a blender or food processor and mix until smooth.
4. Let it cool at room temperature and place it in the fridge for 2–3 hours (or overnight).
5. Pour the mixture in a Pyrex or stainless steel 9x13 pan and freeze for 30 minutes. The edges should start freezing.
6. Using a handheld electric mixer, beat the sorbet for 1 minute, or until smooth.
7. Return the sorbet to the freezer for another 30 minutes and beat again as before. Repeat this step 4–5 times, until the sorbet is firm.
8. Serve right away or transfer the sorbet to an airtight freezer-safe container.

Pineapple Sorbet

Prep time: 5 minutes | Cook time: 5 minutes | Serves 1

- 12 ounces canned pineapple

1. Pour the pineapple, with the liquid from the can, into a ninja CREAMi Pint container and freeze on a level surface in a cold freezer for a full 24 hours.
2. After 24 hours, remove the Pint from the freezer. Remove the lid.
3. Place the Ninja CREAMi Pint into the outer bowl. Place the outer bowl with the Pint in it into the ninja CREAMi machine and turn until the outer bowl locks into place. Push the SORBET button. During the SORBET function, the sorbet will mix together and become very creamy. This should take approximately 2 minutes.
4. Once the SORBET function has ended, turn the outer bowl and release it from the ninja CREAMi machine.
5. Your sorbet is ready to eat! Enjoy!

Honeydew Melon Sorbet

Prep time: 5 minutes | Cook time:5 minutes |Serves 4

- ¼ cup granulated sugar
- ¼ cup water
- 1 tablespoon lemon juice
- 3 cups honeydew melon

1. In a saucepan over medium heat, combine the water and sugar and bring it to a boil.
2. Cook for about 5 minutes, and then remove it from the heat. Stir in the lemon juice. Let it cool completely.
3. Place the honeydew melon in a blender or food processor and mix until smooth. Add the cooled simple syrup and mix to combine.
4. Refrigerate for 2–3 hours, or overnight.
5. Pour the mixture in a Pyrex or stainless steel 9x13 pan and freeze for 30 minutes.
6. Using a handheld electric mixer, beat the sorbet for 1 minute to break up the mixture.
7. Return to the freezer for another 30 minutes and beat again as before. Do this 4–5 times, until the sorbet is firm.
8. Serve right away or transfer the sorbet to an airtight freezer-safe container.

Mango Sorbet

Prep time: 5 minutes | Cook time: 3 minutes |Serves 4

- 5 cups diced mango
- ½ cup sugar
- ¼ cup water
- 1 teaspoon lemon juice

1. In a blender or food processor, place the diced mango, the sugar, water, and lemon juice.
2. Purée until smooth, about 3 minutes.
3. Pour the mixture in a Pyrex or stainless steel 9x13 pan and freeze for 30 minutes. The edges should start freezing.
4. Using a handheld electric mixer, beat the sorbet for 1 minute, or until smooth.
5. Return the sorbet to the freezer for another 30 minutes and beat again as before. Repeat this step 4–5 times, until the sorbet is firm.
6. Serve right away or transfer the sorbet to an airtight freezer-safe container.

Mixed Berries Sorbet

Prep time: 5 minutes | Cook time: 5 minutes | Serves 4

- 1 cup blueberries
- 1 cup raspberries
- 1 cup strawberries, hulled and quartered

1. In an empty Ninja CREAMi pint container, place the berries and with a potato masher, mash until well combined.
2. Cover the container with storage lid and freeze for 24 hours.
3. After 24 hours, remove the lid from container and arrange into the outer bowl of Ninja CREAMi.
4. Install the Creamerizer Paddle onto the lid of Outer Bowl.
5. Then rotate the lid clockwise to lock.
6. Press Power button to turn on the unit.
7. Then press Sorbet button.
8. When the program is completed, turn the Outer Bowl and release it from the machine.
9. Transfer the sorbet into serving bowls and serve immediately.

Kiwi & Strawberry Sorbet

Prep time: 10 minutes | Cook time: 15 minutes | Freeze time: 24 hours | Serves 4

- 2 cups frozen sliced strawberries
- 4 kiwis, peeled and cut into 1-inch pieces
- ¼ cup agave nectar
- ¼ cup water

1. In a high-speed blender, add all the ingredients and pulse until smooth.
2. Transfer the mixture into an empty Ninja CREAMi pint container.
3. Cover the container with storage lid and freeze for 24 hours.
4. After 24 hours, remove the lid from container and arrange into the Outer Bowl of Ninja CREAMi.
5. Install the Creamerizer Paddle onto the lid of Outer Bowl.
6. Then rotate the lid clockwise to lock.
7. Press Power button to turn on the unit.
8. Then press Sorbet button.
9. When the program is completed, turn the Outer Bowl and release it from the machine.
10. Transfer the sorbet into serving bowls and serve immediately.

Grape Sorbet

Prep time: 10 minutes | Cook time: 15 minutes | Freeze time: 24 hours | Serves 4

- ¾ cup frozen grape juice concentrate
- 1½ cups water
- 1 tablespoon fresh lemon juice

1. In a bowl, add all the ingredients and beat until well combined.
2. Transfer the mixture into an empty Ninja CREAMi pint container.
3. Cover the container with storage lid and freeze for 24 hours.
4. After 24 hours, remove the lid from container and arrange into the Outer Bowl of Ninja CREAMi.
5. Install the Creamerizer Paddle onto the lid of Outer Bowl.
6. Then rotate the lid clockwise to lock.
7. Press Power button to turn on the unit.
8. Then press Sorbet button.
9. When the program is completed, turn the Outer Bowl and release it from the machine.
10. Transfer the sorbet into serving bowls and serve immediately.

Cantaloupe Sorbet

Prep time: 5 minutes | Cook time: 10 minutes | Serves 4

- 3 cups cantaloupe pieces
- ⅓ cup water
- ⅓ cup organic sugar
- 1 tablespoon freshly squeezed lemon juice

1. Combine the cantaloupe, water, sugar, and lemon juice in a blender. Blend on high until smooth.
2. Pour the base into a clean CREAMi Pint. Place the storage lid on the container and freeze for 24 hours.
3. Remove the pint from the freezer and take off the lid. Place the pint in the outer bowl of your Ninja CREAMi, install the Creamerizer Paddle in the outer bowl lid, and lock the lid assembly onto the outer bowl. Place the bowl assembly on the motor base, and twist the handle to the right to raise the platform and lock it in place. Select the Sorbet function.
4. Once the machine has finished processing, remove the sorbet from the pint. Serve immediately.

Pomegranate & Blueberry Sorbet

Prep time: 10 minutes | Cook time: 15 minutes | Freeze time: 24 hours | Serves 4

- 1 (15-ounce) can blueberries in light syrup
- ½ cup pomegranate juice

1. In an empty Ninja CREAMi pint container, place the blueberries and top with syrup
2. Add in the pomegranate juice and stir to combine.
3. Cover the container with storage lid and freeze for 24 hours.
4. After 24 hours, remove the lid from container and arrange into the Outer bowl of Ninja CREAMi.
5. Install the Creamerizer Paddle onto the lid of Outer Bowl.
6. Then rotate the lid clockwise to lock.
7. Press Power button to turn on the unit.
8. Then press Sorbet button.
9. When the program is completed, turn the Outer Bowl and release it from the machine.
10. Transfer the sorbet into serving bowls and serve immediately.

Healthy Strawberry Shake

Prep time: 5 minutes | Cook time: 10 minutes | Serves 1

- 1 cup milk
- 1 tablespoon honey
- ½ teaspoon vanilla extract
- ½ cup frozen strawberries

1. Add the milk, honey, vanilla extract, and strawberries into an empty CREAMi Pint.
2. Place Pint in outer bowl, install Creamerizer Paddle onto outer bowl lid and lock the lid assembly on the outer bowl. Place the bowl assembly on the motor base and crank the lever to elevate and secure the platform in place.
3. Select MILKSHAKE.
4. Remove the milkshake from the Pint after the processing is finished.

Salted Caramel Pretzel Milkshake

Prep time: 2 minutes | Cook time: 10 minutes | Serves 2

- 1½ cups vanilla ice cream
- ½ cup whole milk
- 2 tablespoons caramel sauce
- ⅓ cup pretzels, broken
- 2 pinches sea salt

1. Fill an empty CREAMi Pint with the ice cream.
2. Create a 1-inch wide hole in the bottom of the pint using a spoon. Fill the hole with the remaining ingredients.
3. Arrange the pint into the outer bowl of the Ninja CREAMi.
4. Install the Creamerizer Paddle onto the lid of the outer bowl, then rotate the lid clockwise to lock.
5. Turn on the unit.
6. Press the MILKSHAKE button.
7. When the program is complete, turn the outer bowl and release it from the machine.
8. Transfer the shake into serving glasses and serve immediately.

Almond Candy Bar Milkshake

Prep time: 2 minutes | Cook time: 10 minutes | Serves 2

- 1½ cups coconut dulce de leche ice cream
- ½ cup almond milk
- 2 tablespoons almonds, toasted and chopped
- 2 tablespoons vegan chocolate chips
- 2 tablespoons shredded coconut

1. Place all the ingredients in an empty Ninja CREAMi Pint and mix well.
2. Place the pint into the outer bowl of the Ninja CREAMi.
3. Install the Creamerizer Paddle onto the lid of the outer bowl, then rotate the lid clockwise to lock.
4. Turn on the unit.
5. Press the MILKSHAKE button.
6. When the program is complete, turn the outer bowl and release it from the machine.
7. Transfer the shake into serving glasses and serve immediately.

Chocolate & Coffee Milkshake

Prep time: 5 minutes | Cook time: 10 minutes | Serves 1

- 1 ½ cups chocolate ice cream
- ¼ cup tahini
- ½ cup oat milk
- 1 tablespoon chocolate fudge
- 2 tablespoons coffee

1. Add the ice cream to the Ninja Creami pint container.
2. Create a hole in the middle of the ice cream using a spoon.
3. Add the rest of the ingredients to the hole.
4. Lock the container in place inside the machine.
5. Choose Milkshake mode.

Mixed Berries Milkshake

Prep time: 5 minutes | Cook time: 3 minutes | Serves 2

- 1½ cups vanilla ice cream
- ½ cup milk
- ½ cup fresh mixed berries

1. In an empty Ninja CREAMi pint container, place ice cream followed by milk and berries.
2. Arrange the container into the outer bowl of Ninja CREAMi.
3. Install the Creamerizer Paddle onto the lid of Outer Bowl.
4. Then rotate the lid clockwise to lock.
5. Press Power button to turn on the unit.
6. Then press Milkshake button.
7. When the program is completed, turn the Outer Bowl and release it from the machine.
8. Transfer the shake into serving glasses and serve immediately.

Lite Peanut Butter Ice Cream

Prep time: 5 minutes | Cook time: 3 minutes | Serves 4

- 1¾ cups fat-free (skim) milk
- ¼ cup stevia–cane sugar blend
- 1 teaspoon vanilla extract
- 3 tablespoons smooth peanut butter

1. In a medium bowl, whisk together the milk, stevia blend, vanilla extract, and peanut butter until the mixture is smooth and the stevia is fully dissolved. Let the mixture sit for about 5 minutes, until any foam subsides. If the stevia is still not dissolved, whisk again.
2. Pour the base into a clean CREAMi Pint. Place the storage lid on the container and freeze for 24 hours.
3. Remove the pint from the freezer and take off the lid. Place the pint in the outer bowl of your Ninja CREAMi, install the Creamerizer Paddle in the outer bowl lid, and lock the lid assembly onto the outer bowl. Place the bowl assembly on the motor base, and twist the handle to the right to raise the platform and lock it in place. Select the Lite Ice Cream function.
4. Once the machine has finished processing, remove the ice cream from the pint. Serve immediately.

Vanilla Fig and Cashew Milkshake

Prep time: 5 minutes | Cook time: 5 minutes | Serves 2

- 2 (65 g) figs, cut into small pieces
- 2 scoops (120 g) vanilla ice cream
- 2 tablespoons (15 g) cashew nuts
- 1 cup (250 ml) whole milk
- 4 ice cubes

1. Combine the figs, vanilla ice cream, cashews, and milk in a blender. Process until it becomes smooth.
2. Pour mixture into 2 chilled glasses. Garnish with fig slices, if desired.
3. Serve and enjoy.

Pumpkin Pie Milkshake

Prep time: 5 minutes | Cook time: 5 minutes | Serves 2

- 3/4 cup (185 g) pumpkin puree
- 2 scoops (120 g) vanilla ice cream
- 1 tablespoon (7 g) chopped walnuts
- 1/4 teaspoon (0.5 g) pumpkin pie spice
- 1 cup (250 ml) almond milk, unsweetened
- Pumpkin seeds, for garnish (optional)

1. Combine the pumpkin puree, vanilla ice cream, walnuts, pumpkin pie spice, and almond milk in a blender. Process until it becomes smooth.
2. Pour mixture into 2 chilled glasses. Garnish with some pumpkin seeds, if desired.
3. Serve and enjoy!

Dulce De Leche Milkshake

Prep time: 5 minutes | Cook time: 5 minutes | Serves 2

- 1 cup vanilla or coffee ice cream
- ½ cup milk
- 2 tablespoons sweetened condensed milk
- ¼ teaspoon salt

1. Place all ingredients into an empty CREAMi Pint.
2. Place Pint in outer bowl, install Creamerizer Paddle onto outer bowl lid and lock the lid assembly on the outer bowl. Place the bowl assembly on the motor base and crank the lever to elevate and secure the platform in place.
3. Choose the MILKSHAKE option.
4. Remove the milkshake from the Pint after the function is finished.

Vanilla Lemon Cookie Milkshake

Prep time: 10 minutes | Cook time: 10 minutes | Freeze time: 24 hours | Serves 2

- 3 lemon cream sandwich cookies
- 1½ cups vanilla ice cream
- ¼ cup milk

1. Move the ice cream, cookies, and milk into a CREAMi pint container.
2. Fasten the lid of the pint and freeze for 24 hours.
3. After 24 hours, open the pint, fix it into the outer bowl of Ninja CREAMi along with the 'Creamerizer paddle'
4. Fasten the lid, turn on the 'Power Button', and select the 'MILKSHAKE'' function.
5. Ladle out the shake into serving glasses and serve chilled.

Watermelon Plum and Kiwi Milkshake

Prep time: 5 minutes | Cook time: 5 minutes |Serves 2

- 1 cup (150 g) watermelon, diced
- 1/2 cup (85 g) plum, diced
- 1 medium (85 g) kiwifruit, diced
- 1 cup (250 g) almond milk, unsweetened
- 2 scoops (120 g) vanilla flavored ice cream
- 4 ice cubes

1. Place the watermelon, plum, kiwi fruit, almond milk, ice cream, and ice cubes in a blender. Process until it becomes smooth.
2. Pour into 2 serving glasses. Garnish with a slice of watermelon or kiwi, if desired.
3. Serve and enjoy!

Peanut Butter Banana Milkshake

Prep time: 5 minutes | Cook time: 10 minutes | Freeze time: 24 hours | Serves 2

- ¼ cup peanut butter
- 3 bananas, frozen
- ½ cup coconut milk
- Dash of maple syrup
- Dash of cinnamon

1. Move the peanut butter, bananas, maple syrup, cinnamon, and coconut milk into a CREAMi pint container.
2. Fasten the lid of the pint and freeze for 24 hours.
3. After 24 hours, open the pint, fix it into the outer bowl of Ninja CREAMi along with the 'Creamerizer paddle'
4. Fasten the lid, turn on the 'Power Button', and select the 'MILKSHAKE'' function.
5. Ladle out the shake into serving glasses and serve chilled.

Tahini Chocolate oat Milkshake

Prep time: 5 minutes | Cook time: 10 minutes | Freeze time: 24 hours | Serves 1

- ½ cup oat milk
- 1½ cups chocolate ice cream
- ¼ cup tahini
- 2 tablespoons coffee
- 2 orange slices

1. Move the tahini with the remaining ingredients into a CREAMi pint container except the orange slices.
2. Fasten the lid of the pint and freeze for 24 hours.
3. After 24 hours, open the pint, fix it into the outer bowl of Ninja CREAMi along with the 'Creamerizer paddle'
4. Fasten the lid, turn on the 'Power Button', and select the 'MILKSHAKE'' function.
5. Ladle out the shake into serving glasses and serve topped with orange slices.

Cocoa & Mint Milkshake

Prep time: 5 minutes | Cook time: 10 minutes | Serves 2

- 1 ½ cups vanilla coconut milk ice cream
- ½ cup coconut milk
- 1 teaspoon matcha powder
- ¼ cup cocoa powder
- 1 teaspoon peppermint extract

1. Pour the ice cream into the Ninja Creami pint container.
2. Create a hole in the middle of the ice cream using a spoon.
3. Add the rest of the ingredients to the hole.
4. Place the container in the machine.
5. Choose Milkshake mode.

PER SERVING

Calories: 576 | Protein: 7.45 | Fat: 58.63 | Carbs: 19.6

Strawberry Cake Milkshake

Prep time: 2 minutes | Cook time: 10 minutes | Freeze time: 24 hours | Serves 2

- ½ cup whole milk
- 1½ cups strawberry ice cream
- ¼ premade pound cake, crumbled
- ¼ cup fresh strawberries, trimmed and quartered

1. Move the ice cream into a CREAMi pint container.
2. Make a broad hole in the bottom of the pint and fill it with the milk, strawberries, and pound cake.
3. Fasten the lid of the pint and freeze for 24 hours.
4. After 24 hours, open the pint, fix it into the outer bowl of Ninja CREAMi along with the 'Creamerizer paddle'
5. Fasten the lid, turn on the 'Power Button', and select the 'MILKSHAKE" function.
6. Ladle out the shake into serving glasses and serve chilled.

Chocolate Cherry Milkshake

Prep time: 10 minutes | Cook time: 10 minutes | Serves 2

- 1½ cups chocolate ice cream
- ½ cup canned cherries in syrup, drained
- ¼ cup whole milk

1. In an empty Ninja CREAMi pint container, place ice cream followed by cherries and milk.
2. Arrange the container into the Outer Bowl of Ninja CREAMi.
3. Install the Creamerizer Paddle onto the lid of Outer Bowl.
4. Then rotate the lid clockwise to lock.
5. Press Power button to turn on the unit.
6. Then press Milkshake button.
7. When the program is completed, turn the Outer Bowl and release it from the machine.
8. Transfer the shake into serving glasses and serve immediately.

Cashew Butter Milkshake

Prep time: 10 minutes | Cook time: 10 minutes | Serves 2

- 1½ cups vanilla ice cream
- ½ cup canned cashew milk
- ¼ cup cashew butter

1. In an empty Ninja CREAMi pint container, place the ice cream.
2. With a spoon, create a 1½-inch wide hole in the center that reaches the bottom of the pint container.
3. Add the remaining ingredients into the hole.
4. Arrange the container into the Outer Bowl of Ninja CREAMi.
5. Install the Creamerizer Paddle onto the lid of Outer Bowl.
6. Then rotate the lid clockwise to lock.
7. Press Power button to turn on the unit.
8. Then press Milkshake button.
9. When the program is completed, turn the Outer Bowl and release it from the machine.
10. Transfer the shake into serving glasses and serve immediately.

Rich Chocolate Milkshake

Prep time: 5 minutes | Cook time: 5 minutes | Serves 2

- 2 scoops (120 g) chocolate ice cream
- 1/4 cup (80 g) dark chocolate sauce
- 1 cup (250 ml) whole milk
- 6 ice cubes
- Cocoa powder

1. Place the chocolate ice cream, chocolate sauce, milk, and ice in a high-speed blender. Process until smooth and creamy.
2. Pour into 2 chilled glasses. Sprinkle with cocoa powder, if desired.
3. Serve and enjoy.

Cacao Mint Milkshake

Prep time: 10 minutes | Cook time: 10 minutes | Serves 2

- 1½ cups vanilla ice cream
- ½ cup canned full-fat coconut milk
- 1 teaspoon matcha powder
- ¼ cup cacao nibs
- 1 teaspoon peppermint extract

1. In an empty Ninja CREAMi pint container, place ice cream followed by coconut milk, matcha powder, cacao nibs and peppermint extract.
2. Arrange the container into the Outer Bowl of Ninja CREAMi.
3. Install the Creamerizer Paddle onto the lid of Outer Bowl.
4. Then rotate the lid clockwise to lock.
5. Press Power button to turn on the unit.
6. Then press Milkshake button.
7. When the program is completed, turn the Outer Bowl and release it from the machine.
8. Transfer the shake into serving glasses and serve immediately.

Mint Cookies 'n Sea Salt "Silkshake"

Prep time: 5 minutes | Cook time: 25 minutes | Serves 6

- 2 cups heavy cream
- 1 cup milk
- 3/4 cup sugar
- 1 teaspoon sea salt
- 1 teaspoon vanilla extract
- 1 ½ teaspoons mint extract
- 10 chocolate sandwich cookies

1. Freeze bowl (Refer to note on page XX about freezing bowl)
2. Place the milk and cream in a bowl, and mix them together until well combined. Use a whisk to mix in the sugar. Continue to whisk for about 4 minutes until the sugar dissolves. Then mix in the vanilla, sea salt and mint extract.
3. Place the sandwich cookies in a food processor, and process until the cookies are finely processed. If you don't have a food processor place the cookies in a large resealable plastic bag, and seal it shut. Use your hands, a mallet, or a rolling pin to crush the cookies.
4. Pour the ingredients into your ice cream maker, and let it churn for 10-15 minutes, until desired consistency is reached. About 5 minutes before the ice cream is done churning add the cookies to your ice cream maker.

Blueberry Banana Soy Milkshake

Prep time: 5 minutes | Cook time: 5 minutes | Serves 2

- 1 cup (155 g) frozen blueberries, plus more for garnish
- 1 large (180 g) frozen banana, cut into small pieces
- 1 scoop (60 g) vanilla ice cream
- 1 ½ cups (375 ml) soy milk
- Fresh mint sprigs

1. Place the blueberries, banana, ice cream, and soy milk in a high-speed blender. Process until smooth and creamy.
2. Pour into 2 chilled glasses. Garnish with some blueberries and mint sprigs.
3. Serve and enjoy!

Appendix 1 Measurement Conversion Chart

Volume Equivalents (Dry)

US STANDARD	METRIC (APPROXIMATE)
1/8 teaspoon	0.5 mL
1/4 teaspoon	1 mL
1/2 teaspoon	2 mL
3/4 teaspoon	4 mL
1 teaspoon	5 mL
1 tablespoon	15 mL
1/4 cup	59 mL
1/2 cup	118 mL
3/4 cup	177 mL
1 cup	235 mL
2 cups	475 mL
3 cups	700 mL
4 cups	1 L

Volume Equivalents (Liquid)

US STANDARD	US STANDARD (OUNCES)	METRIC (APPROXIMATE)
2 tablespoons	1 fl.oz.	30 mL
1/4 cup	2 fl.oz.	60 mL
1/2 cup	4 fl.oz.	120 mL
1 cup	8 fl.oz.	240 mL
1 1/2 cup	12 fl.oz.	355 mL
2 cups or 1 pint	16 fl.oz.	475 mL
4 cups or 1 quart	32 fl.oz.	1 L
1 gallon	128 fl.oz.	4 L

Temperatures Equivalents

FAHRENHEIT(F)	CELSIUS(C) APPROXIMATE)
225 °F	107 °C
250 °F	120 ° °C
275 °F	135 °C
300 °F	150 °C
325 °F	160 °C
350 °F	180 °C
375 °F	190 °C
400 °F	205 °C
425 °F	220 °C
450 °F	235 °C
475 °F	245 °C
500 °F	260 °C

Weight Equivalents

US STANDARD	METRIC (APPROXIMATE)
1 ounce	28 g
2 ounces	57 g
5 ounces	142 g
10 ounces	284 g
15 ounces	425 g
16 ounces (1 pound)	455 g
1.5 pounds	680 g
2 pounds	907 g

Appendix 2 The Dirty Dozen and Clean Fifteen

The Environmental Working Group (EWG) is a nonprofit, nonpartisan organization dedicated to protecting human health and the environment Its mission is to empower people to live healthier lives in a healthier environment. This organization publishes an annual list of the twelve kinds of produce, in sequence, that have the highest amount of pesticide residue-the Dirty Dozen-as well as a list of the fifteen kinds ofproduce that have the least amount of pesticide residue-the Clean Fifteen.

THE DIRTY DOZEN	
The 2016 Dirty Dozen includes the following produce. These are considered among the year's most important produce to buy organic:	
Strawberries	Spinach
Apples	Tomatoes
Nectarines	Bell peppers
Peaches	Cherry tomatoes
Celery	Cucumbers
Grapes	Kale/collard greens
Cherries	Hot peppers

The Dirty Dozen list contains two additional itemskale/collard greens and hot peppers-because they tend to contain trace levels of highly hazardous pesticides.

THE CLEAN FIFTEEN	
The least critical to buy organically are the Clean Fifteen list. The following are on the 2016 list:	
Avocados	Papayas
Corn	Kiw
Pineapples	Eggplant
Cabbage	Honeydew
Sweet peas	Grapefruit
Onions	Cantaloupe
Asparagus	Cauliflower
Mangos	

Some of the sweet corn sold in the United States are made from genetically engineered (GE) seedstock. Buy organic varieties of these crops to avoid GE produce.

Appendix 3 Index

EVE P. HOGAN

Printed in the USA
CPSIA information can be obtained
at www.ICGtesting.com
LVHW071005141223
766498LV00011B/300